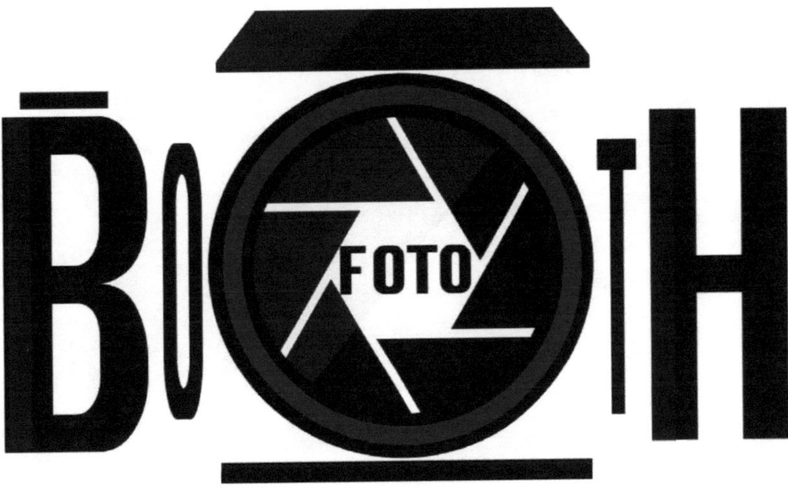

BOOTH
FOTO

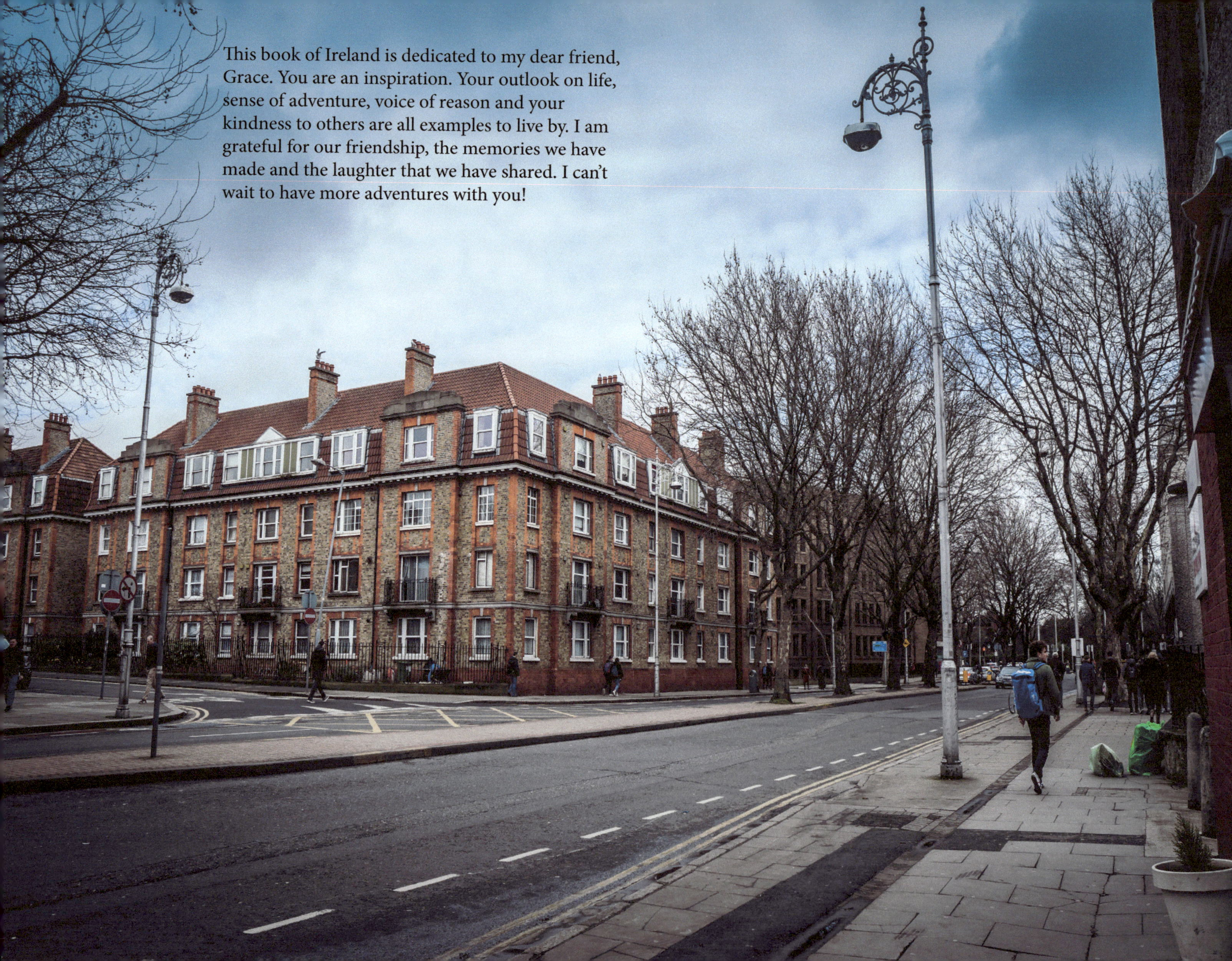

This book of Ireland is dedicated to my dear friend,
Grace. You are an inspiration. Your outlook on life,
sense of adventure, voice of reason and your
kindness to others are all examples to live by. I am
grateful for our friendship, the memories we have
made and the laughter that we have shared. I can't
wait to have more adventures with you!

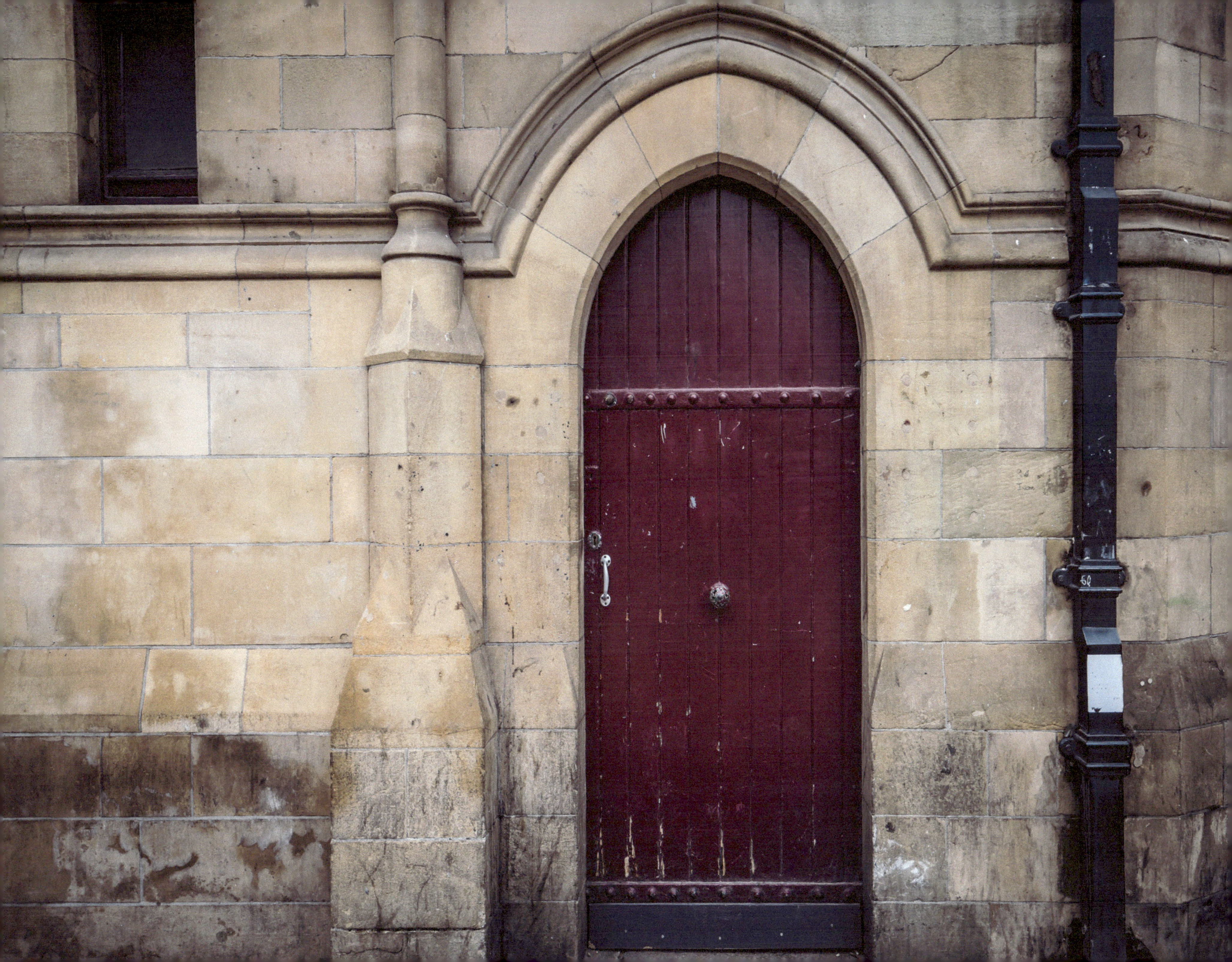

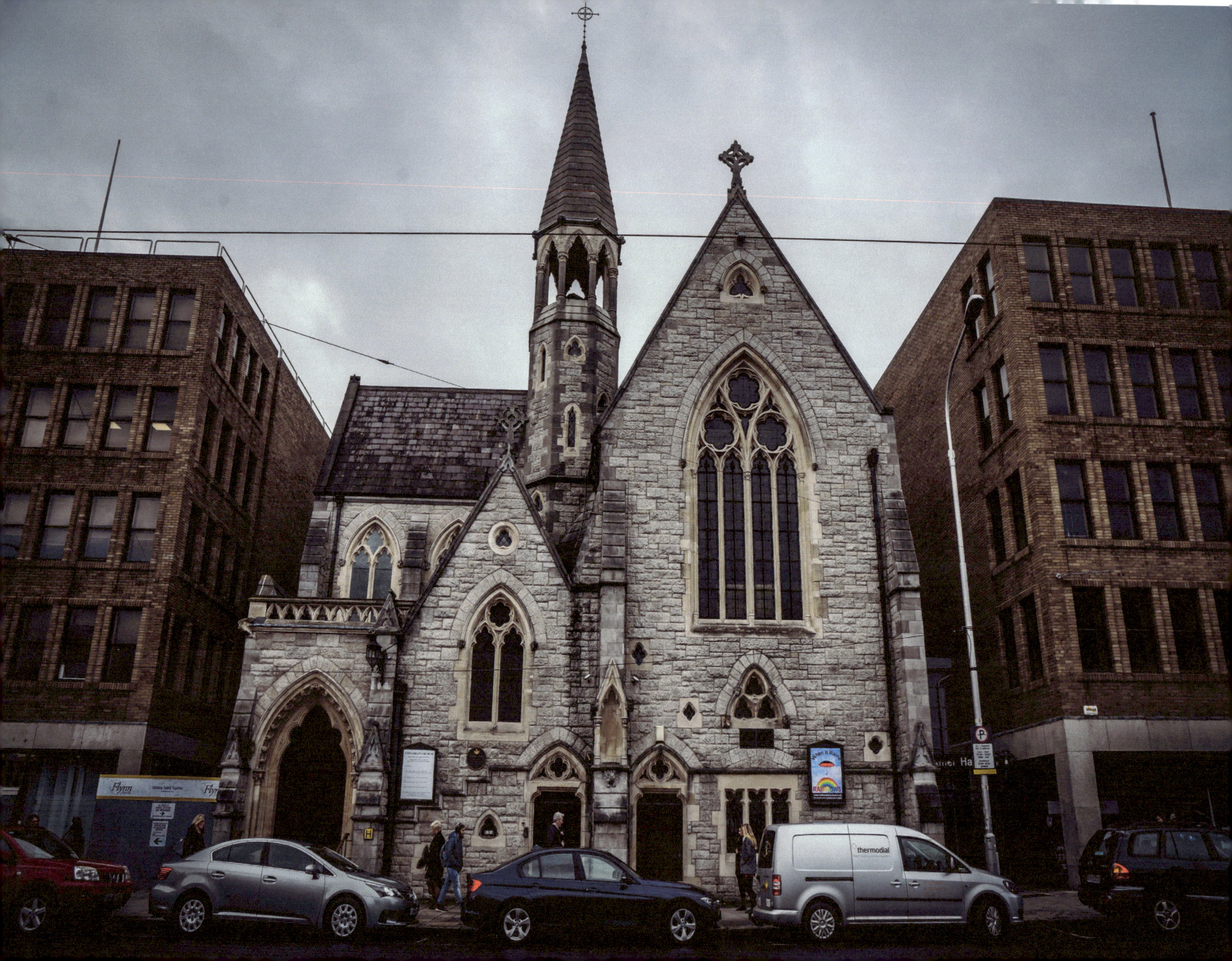

thermodial
RAINBOWS
Flynn

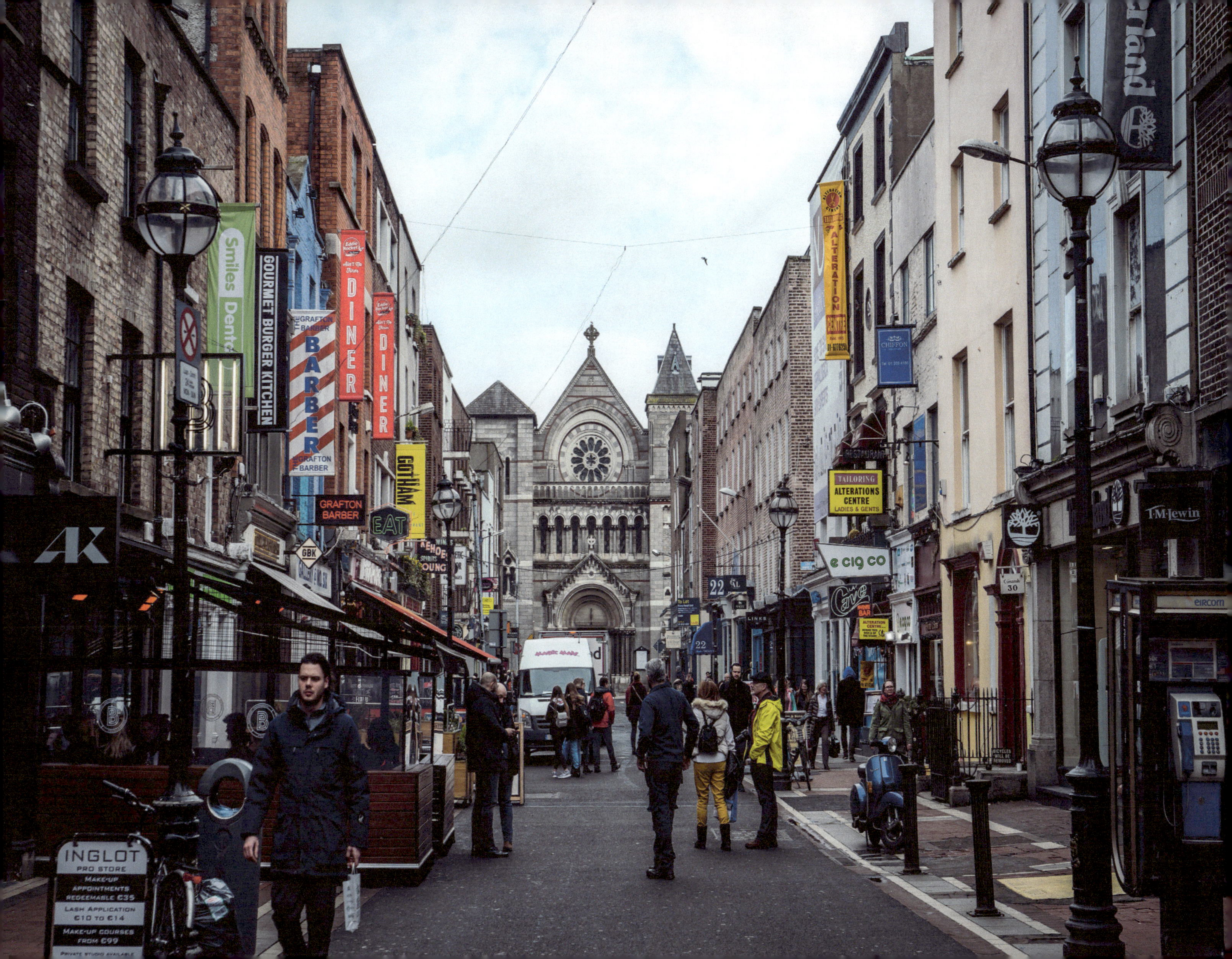
Smiles Dental
GOURMET BURGER KITCHEN
BARBER
GRAFTON BARBER
DINER
DINER
GOTHAM
GRAFTON BARBER
EAT
GBK
AK
ALTERATION CENTRE
CHIFFON
TAILORING
ALTERATIONS
CENTRE
LADIES & GENTS
RESTAURANT
e cig co
T·M·LEWIN
22
30
eircom
INGLOT
PRO STORE
MAKE-UP
APPOINTMENTS
REDEEMABLE €35
LASH APPLICATION
€10 TO €14
MAKE-UP COURSES
FROM €99

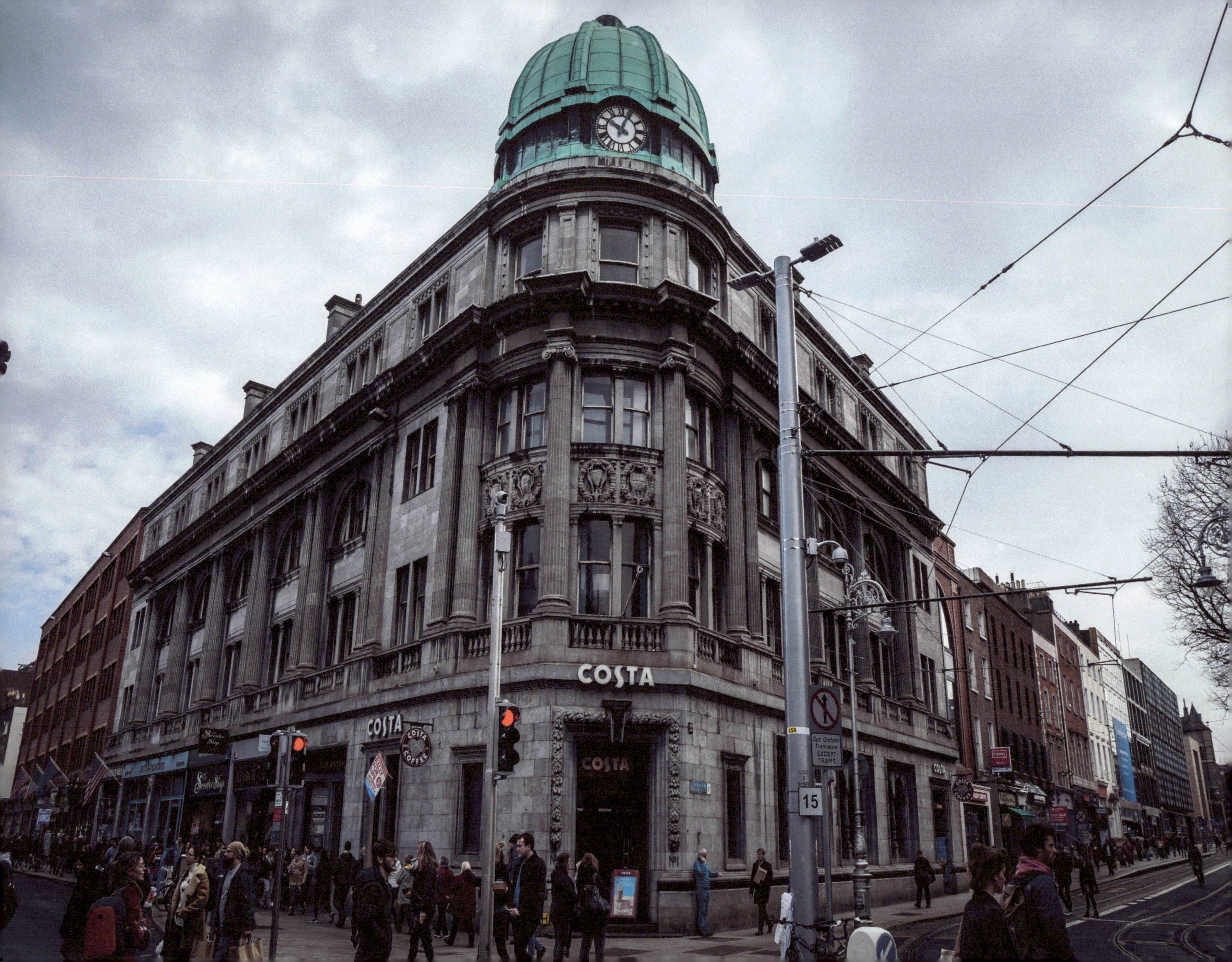
COSTA
COSTA
COSTA COFFEE
COSTA
15

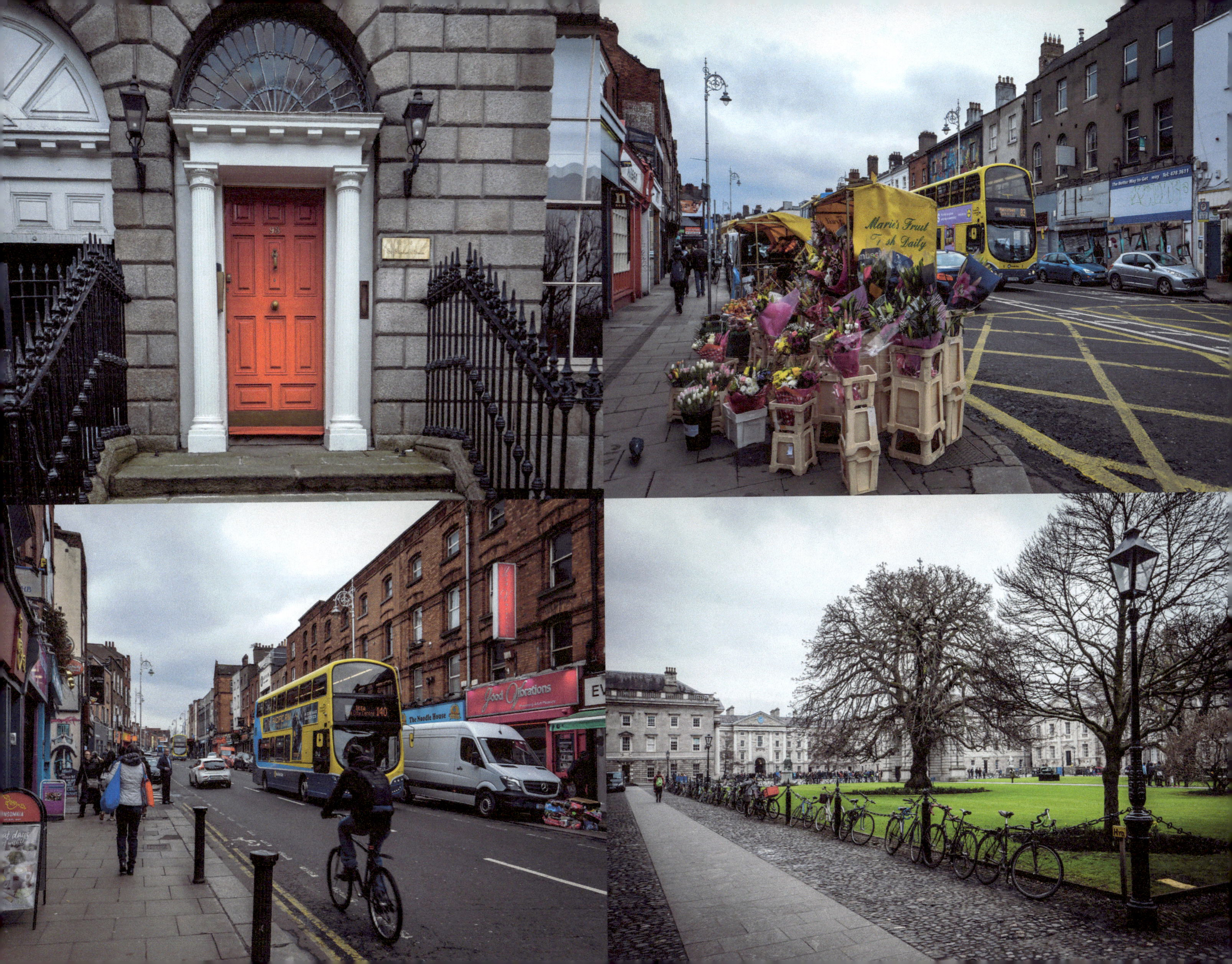

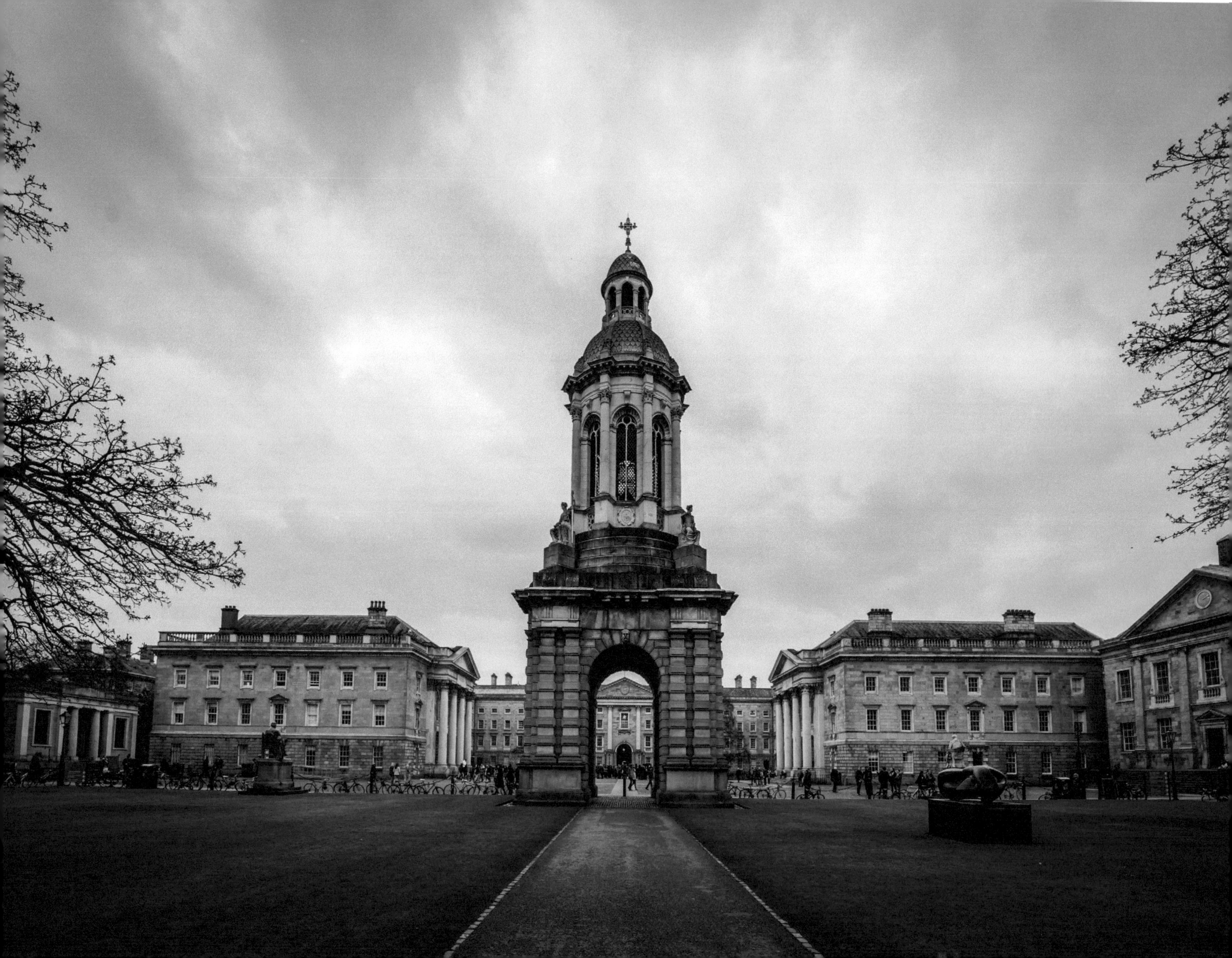

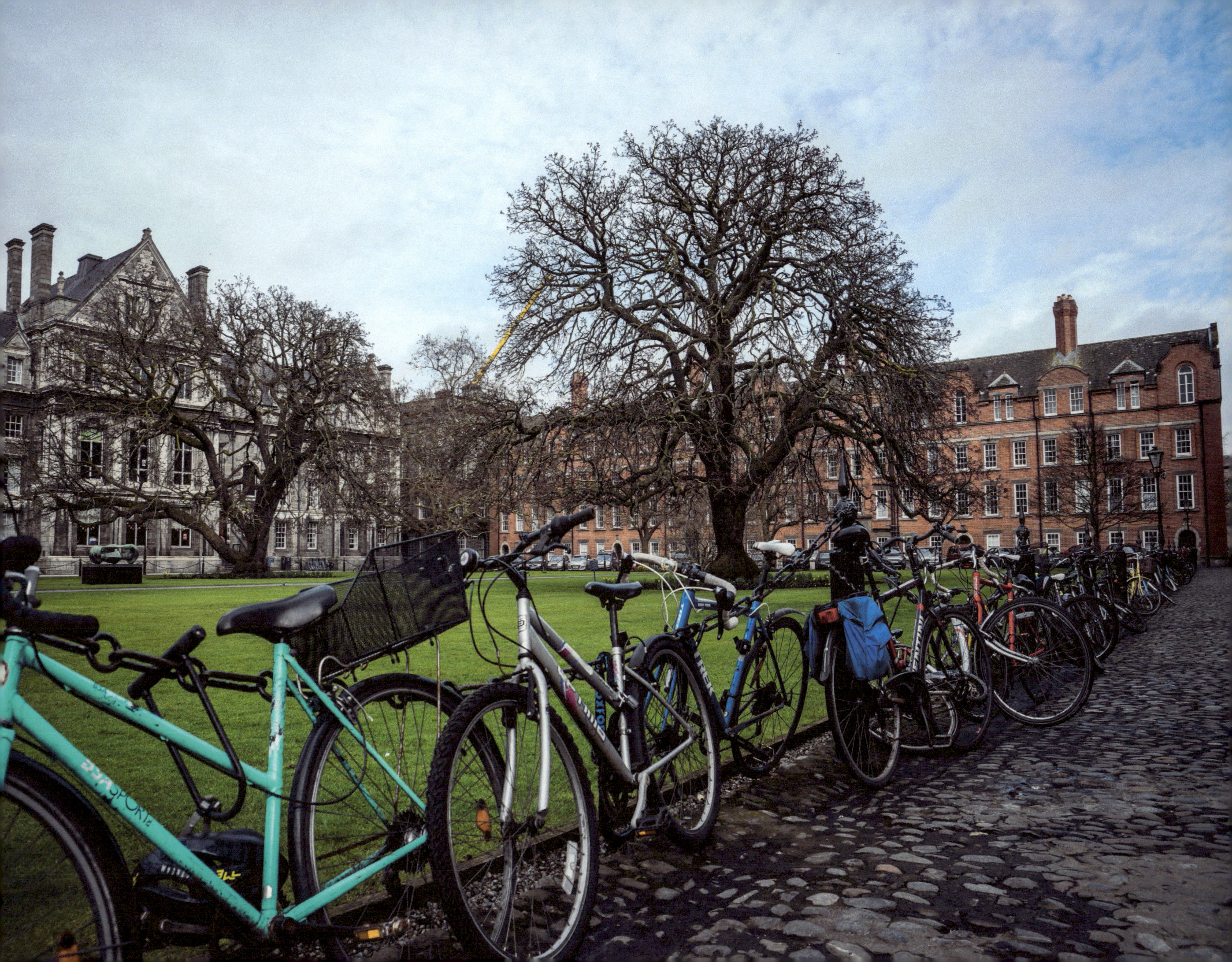

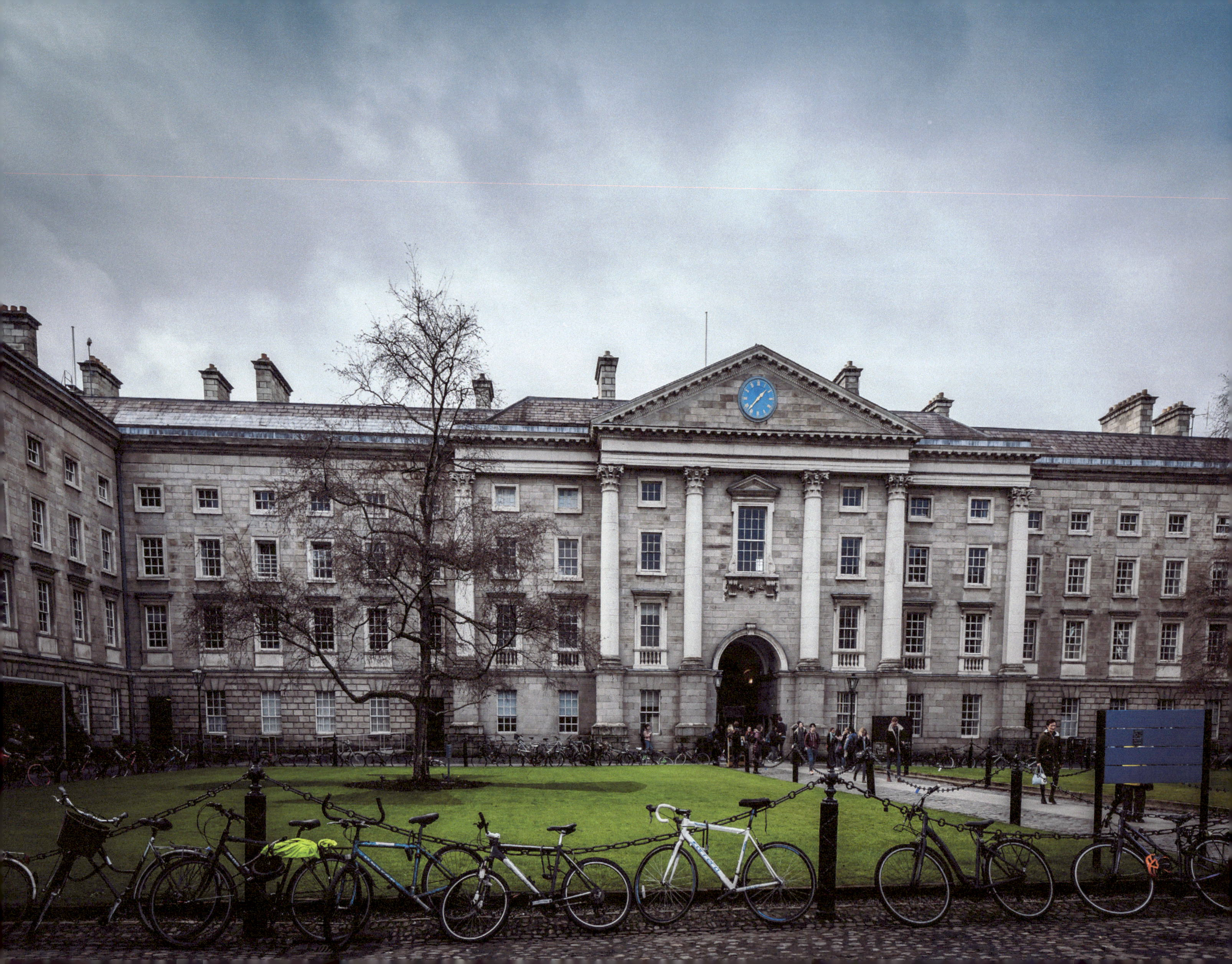

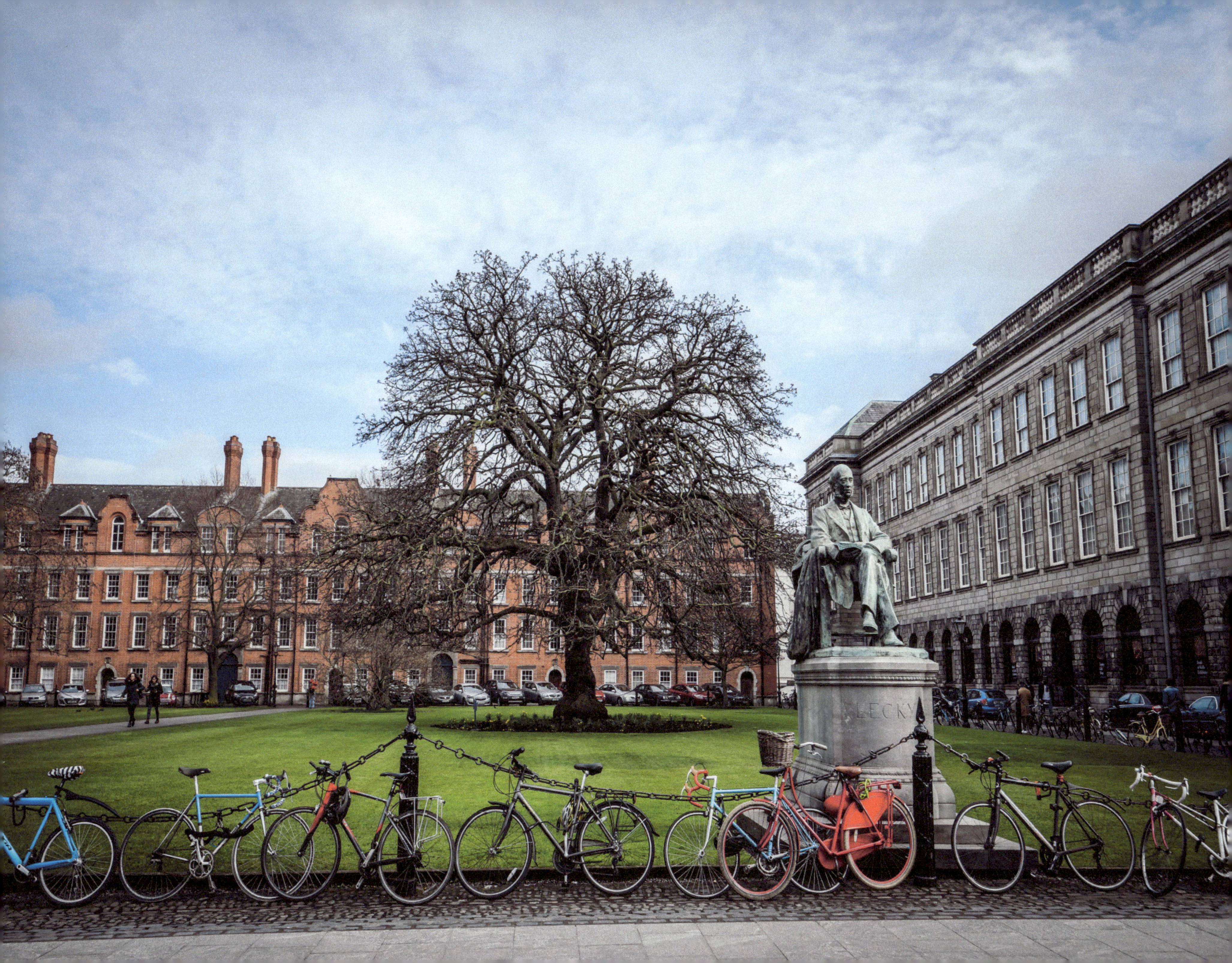

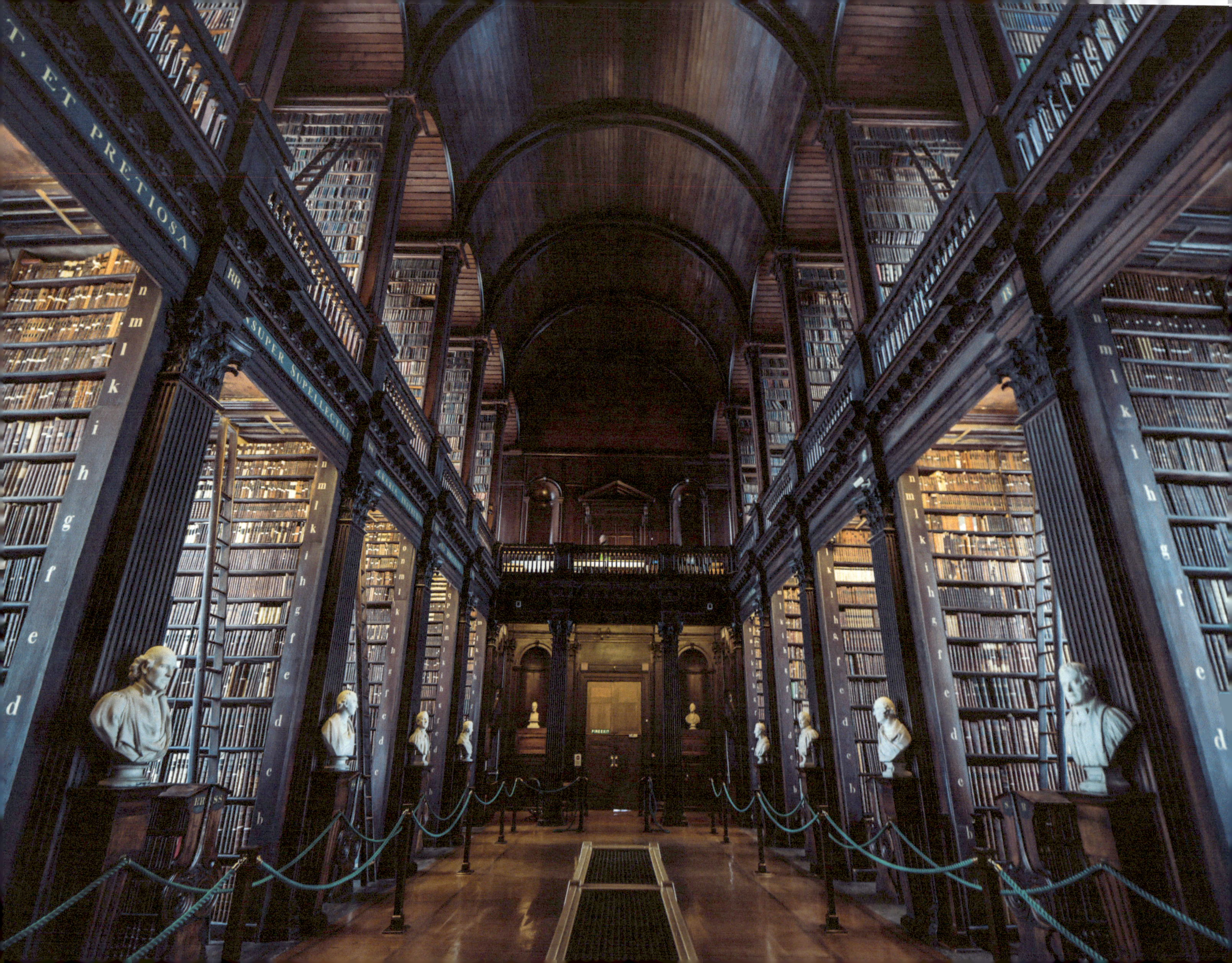

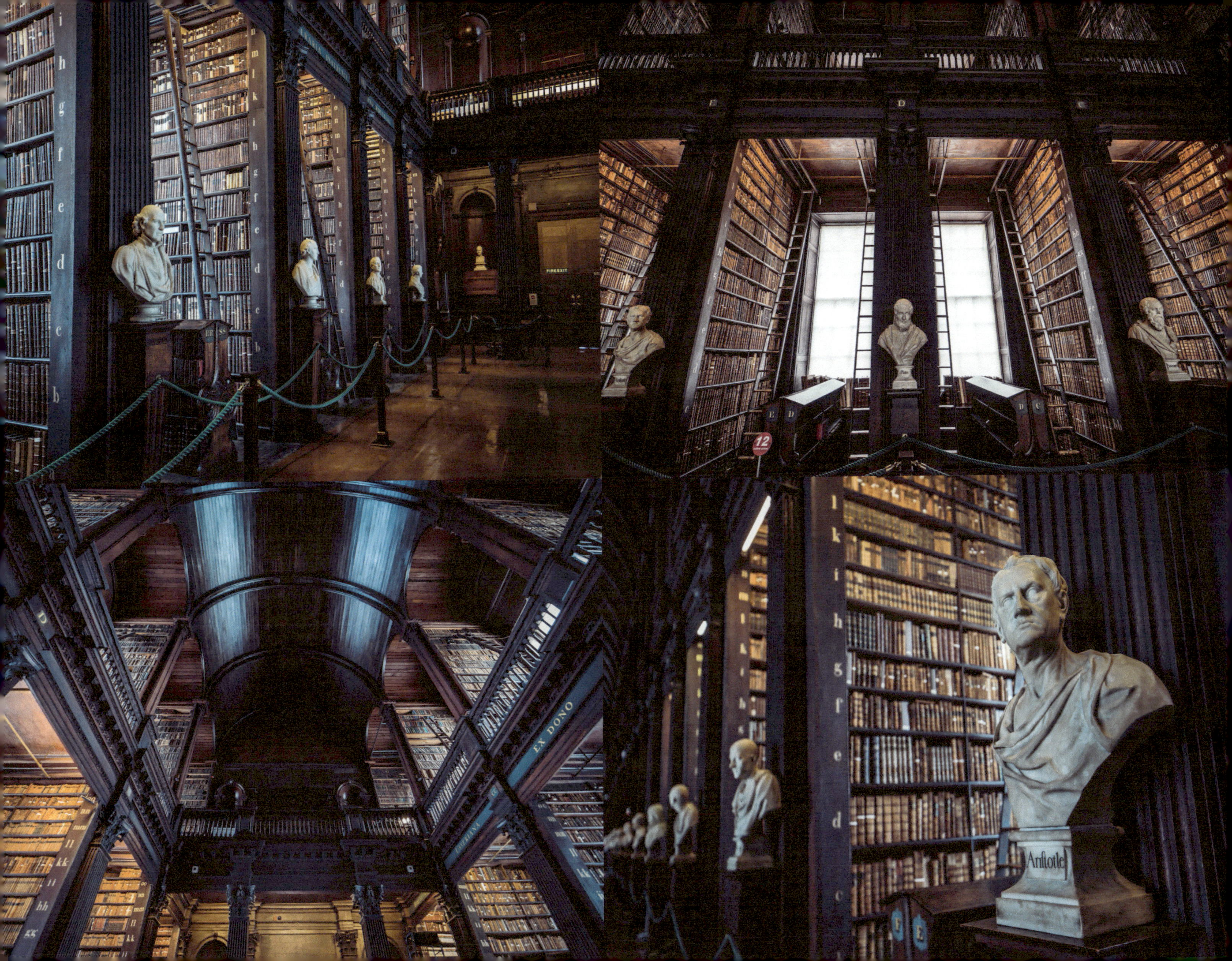
EX DONO
Ariftotle

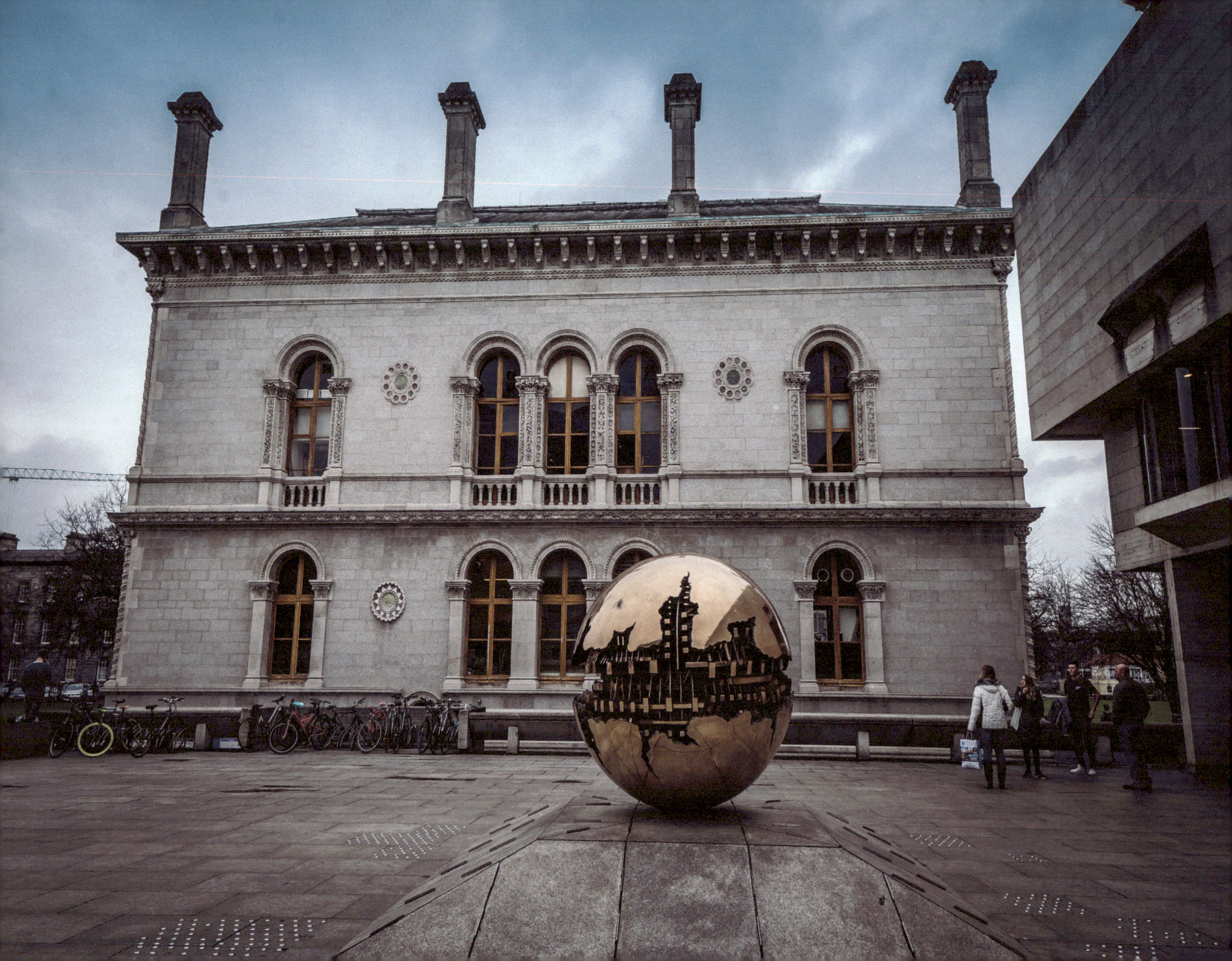

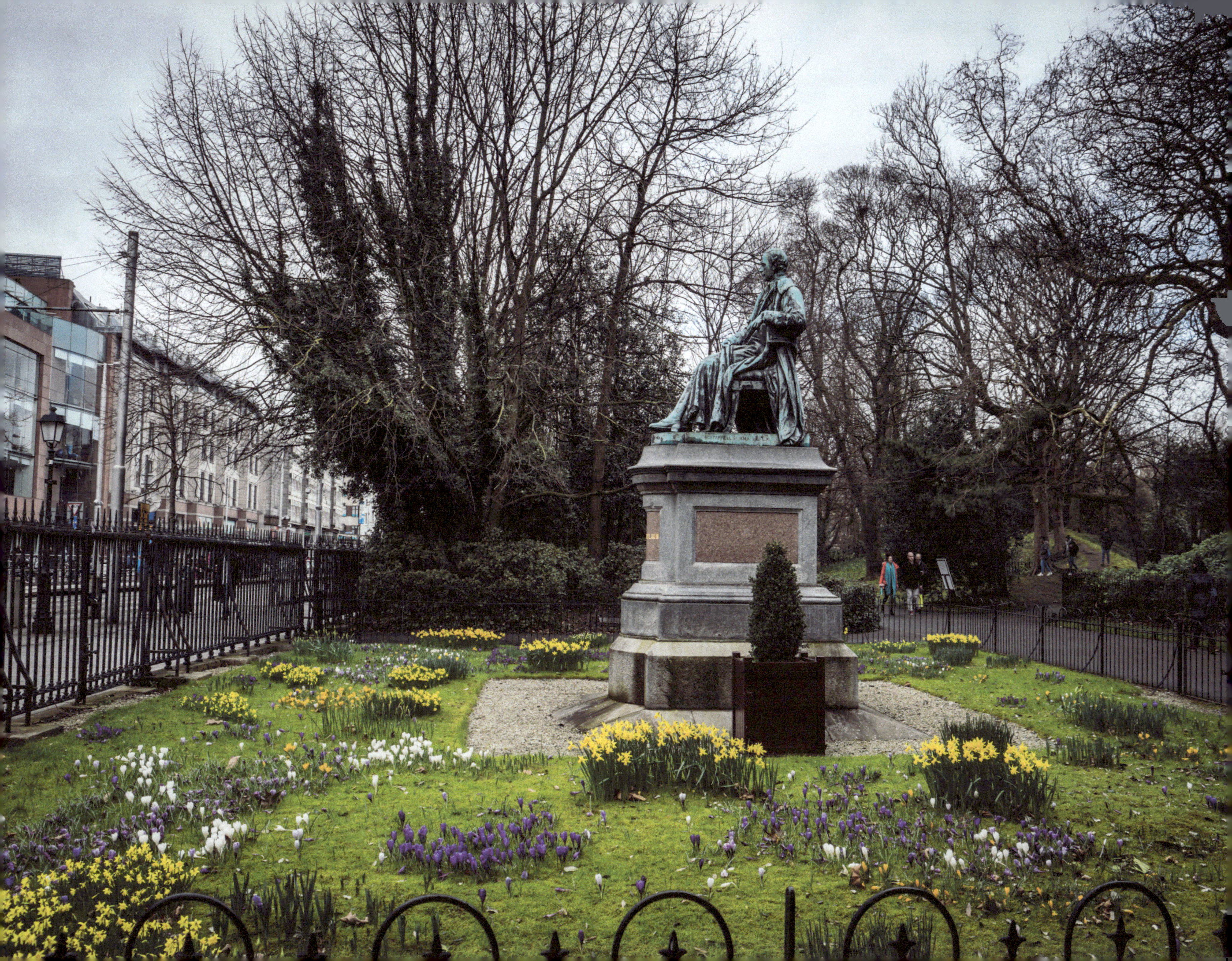

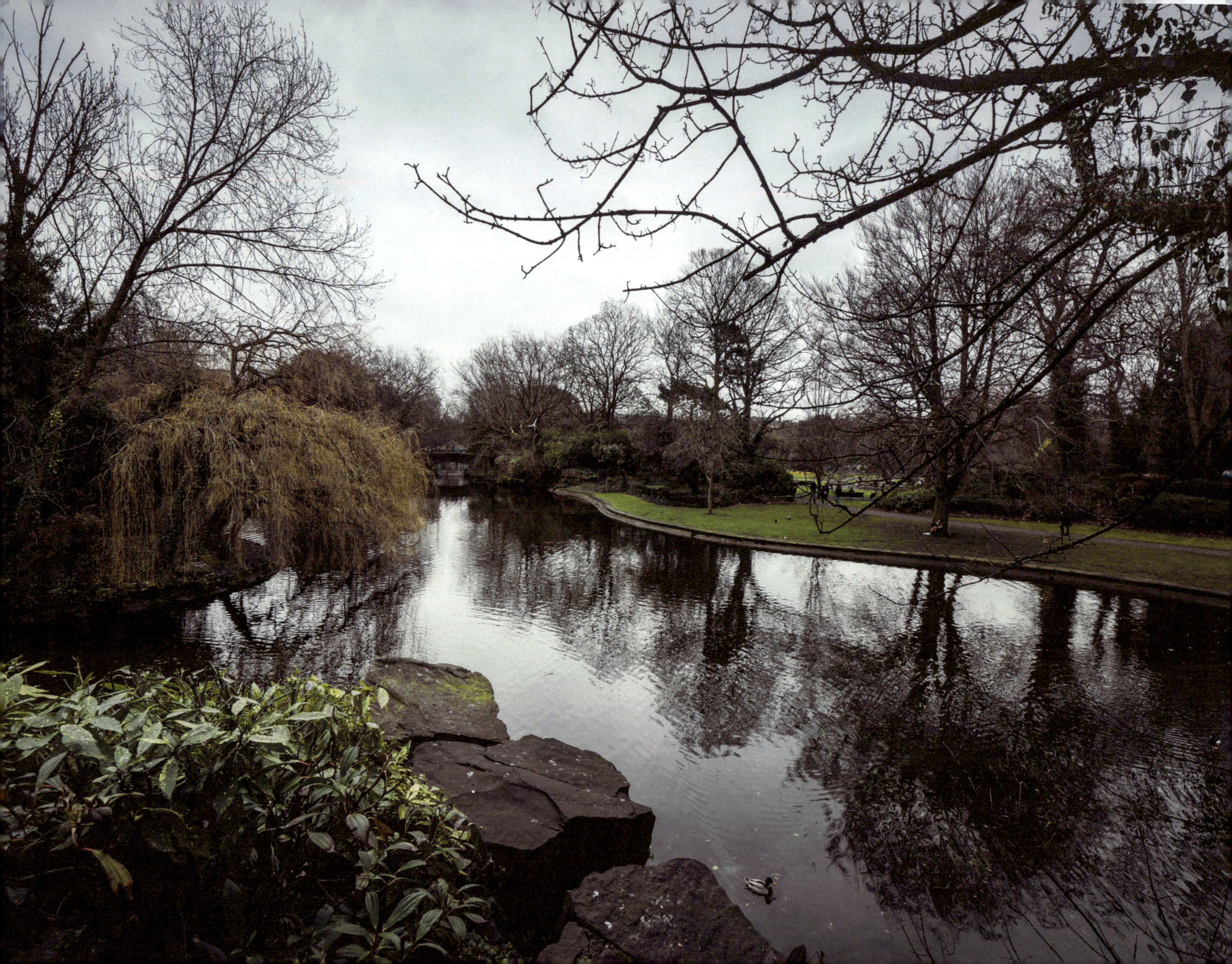

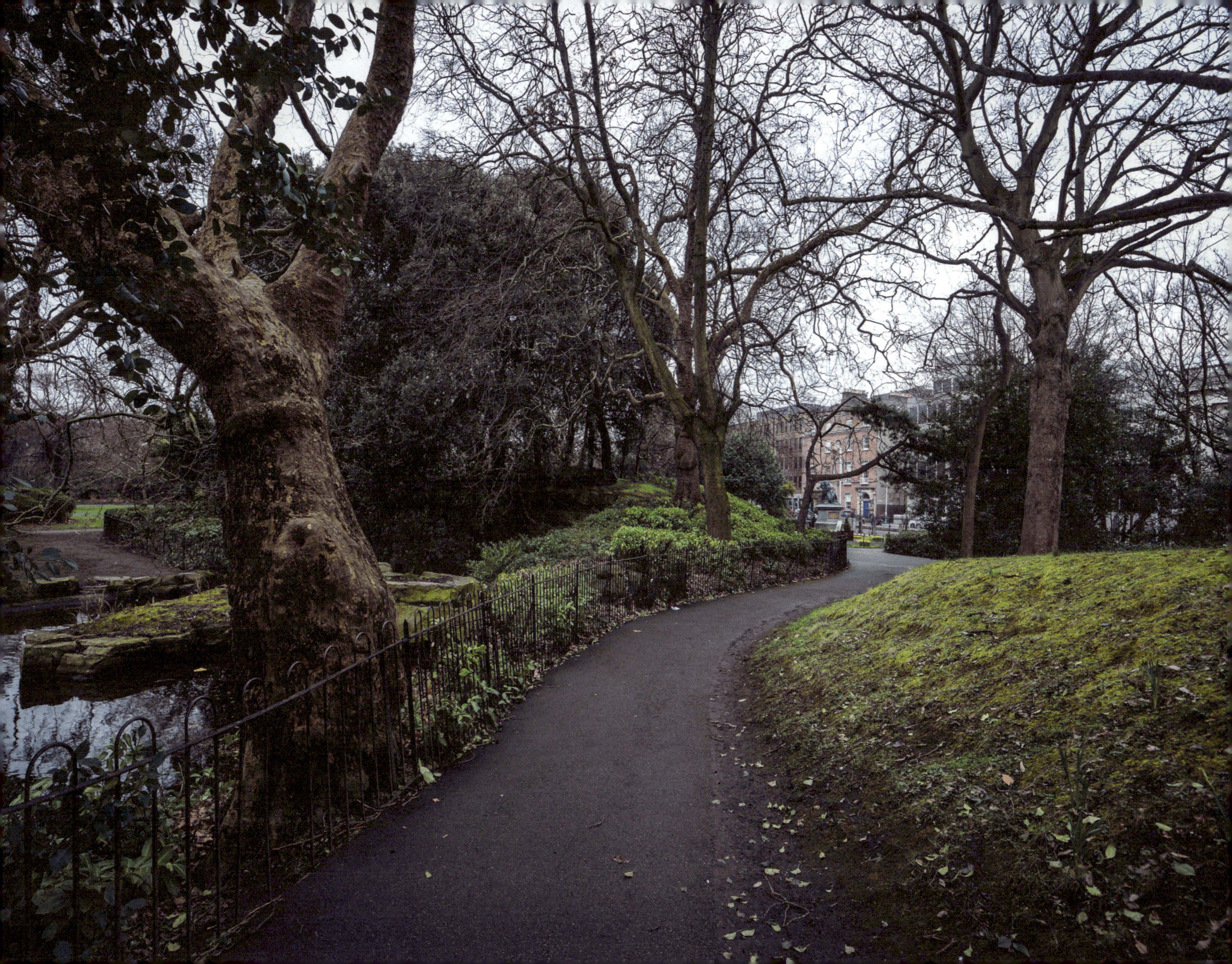

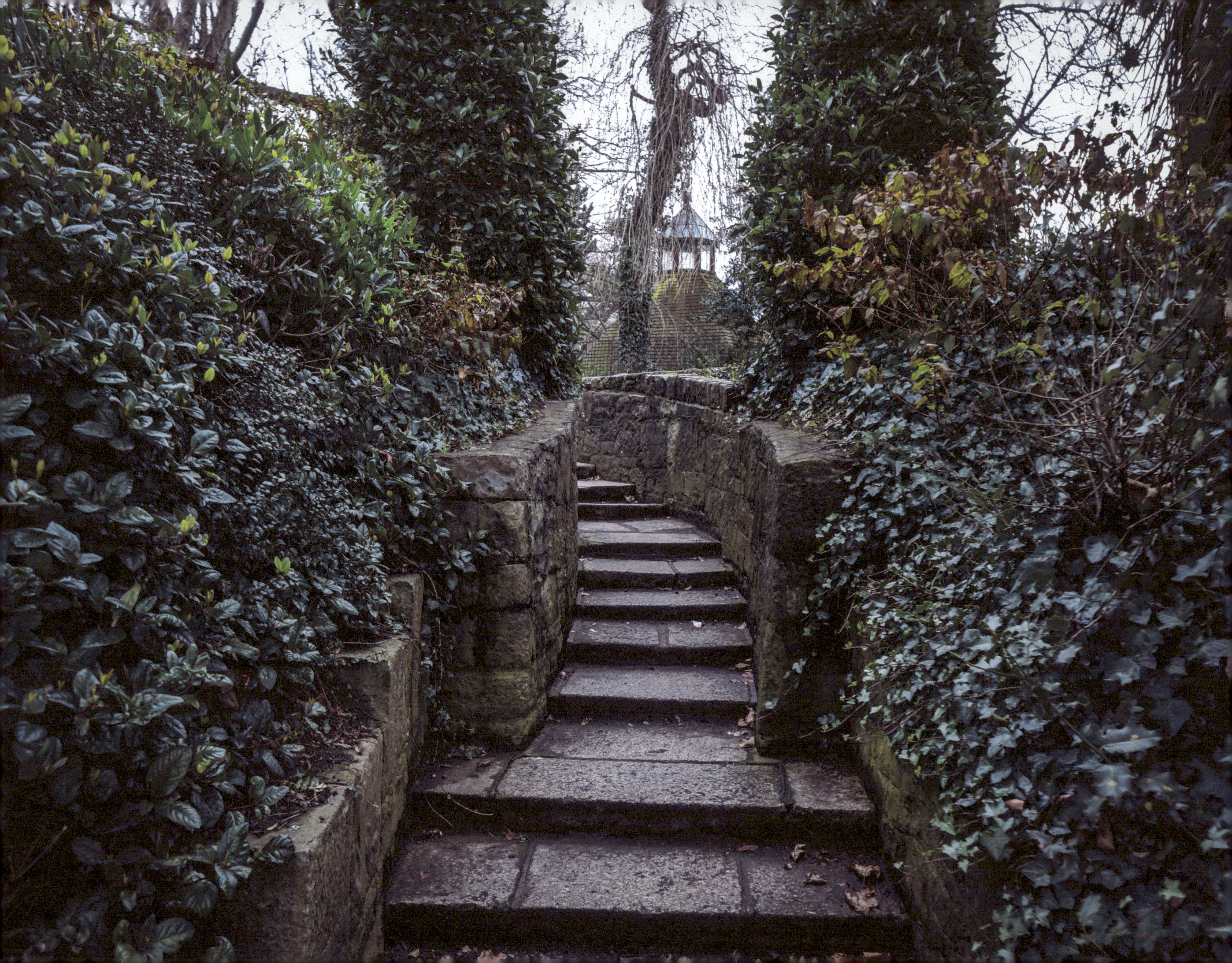

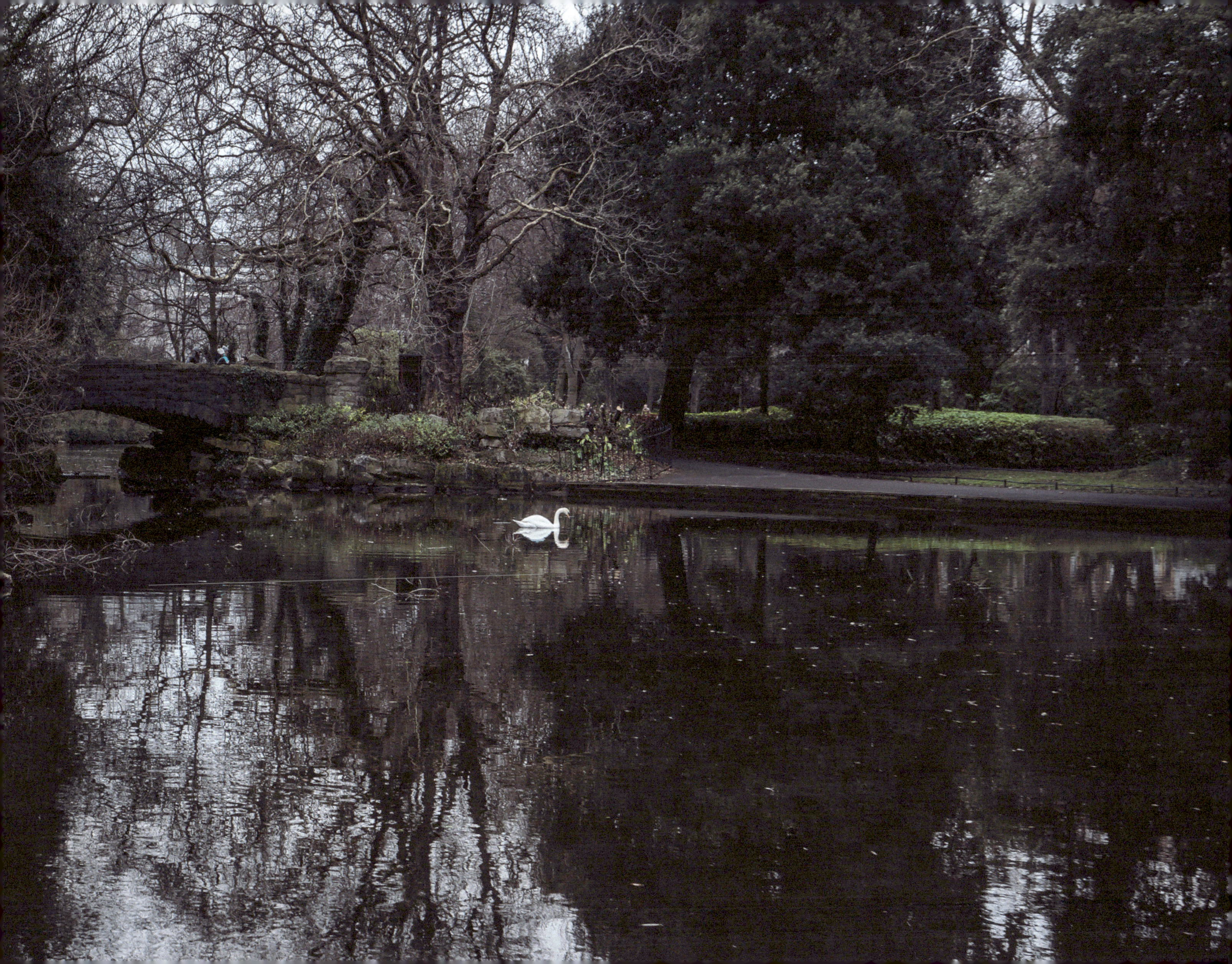

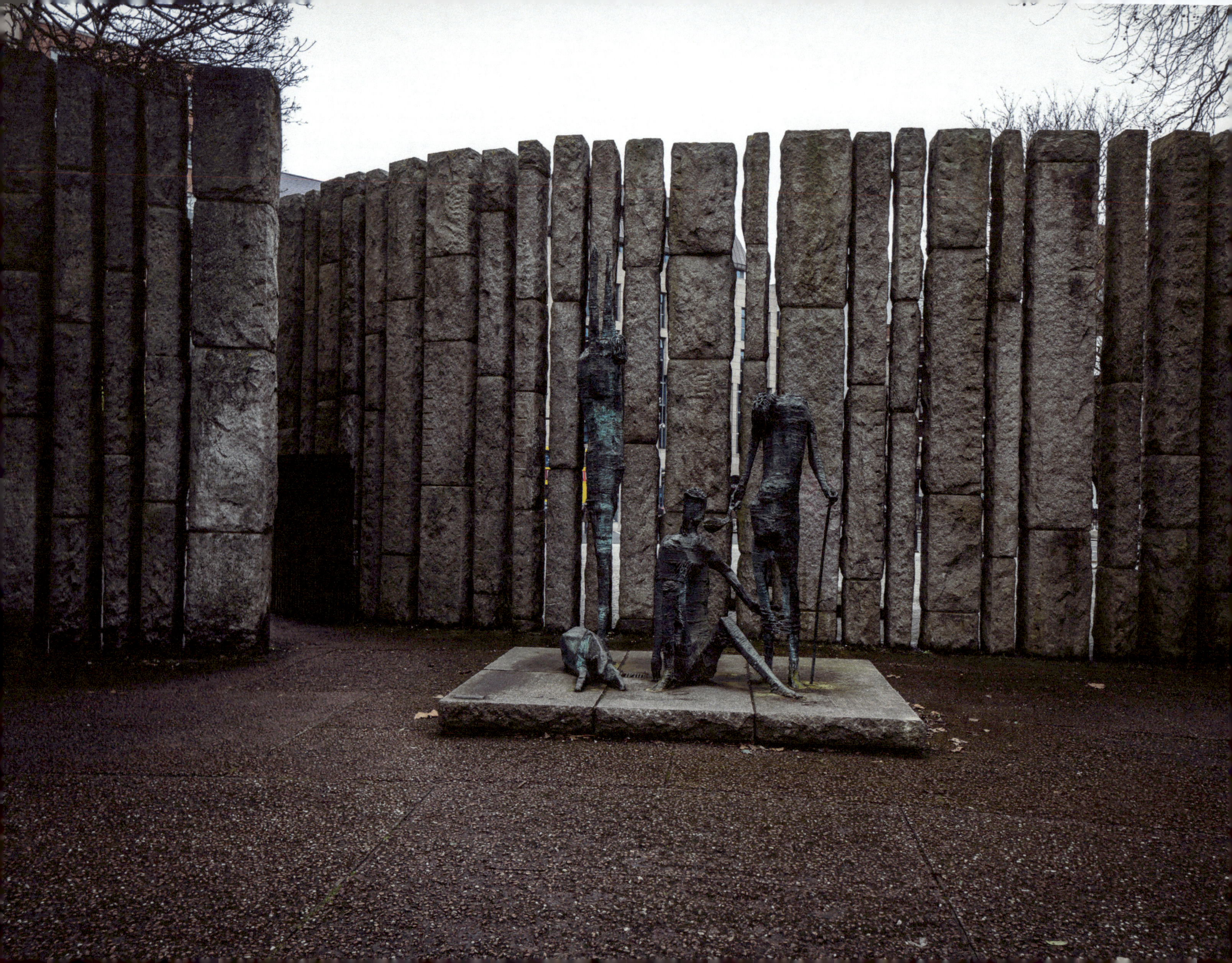

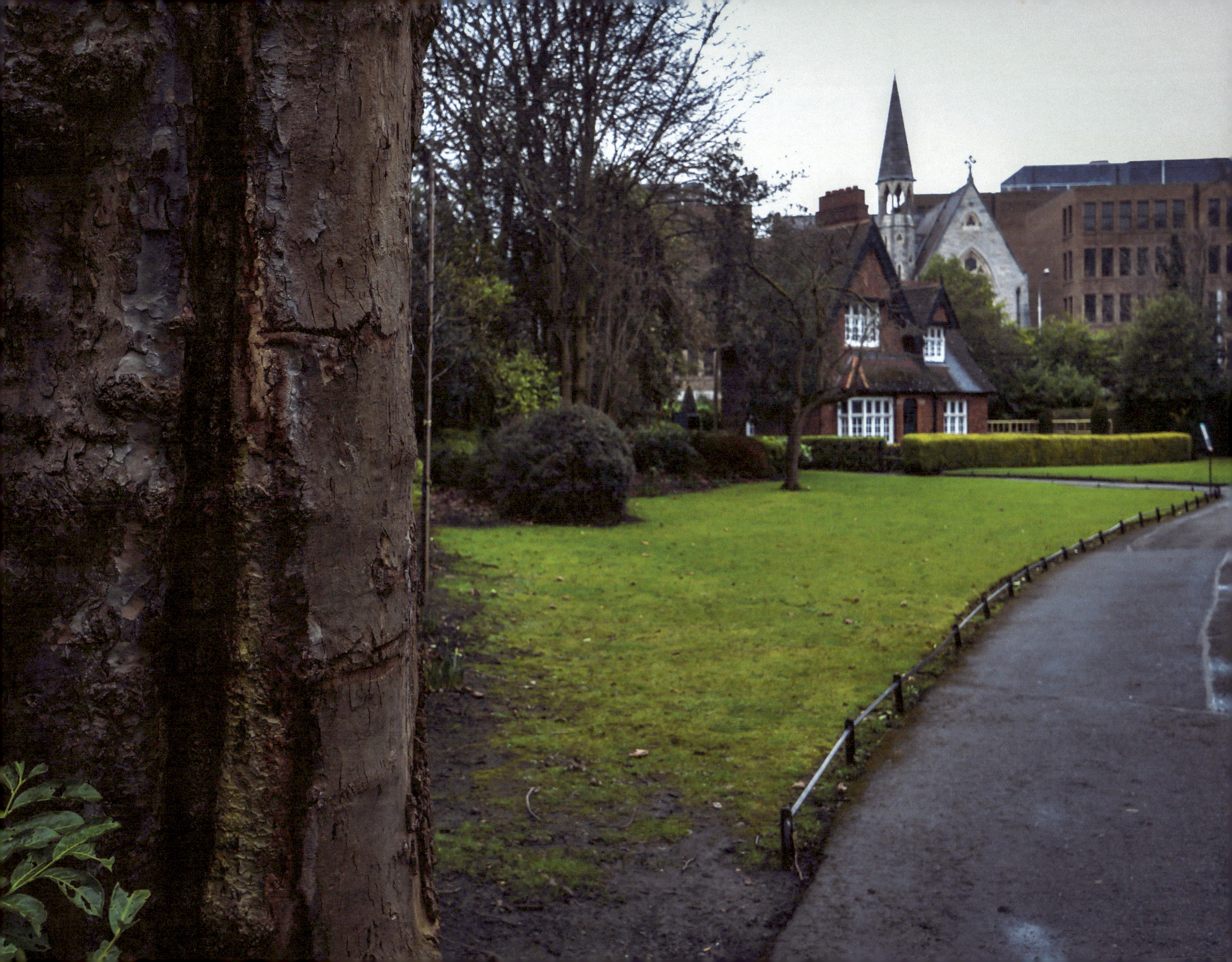

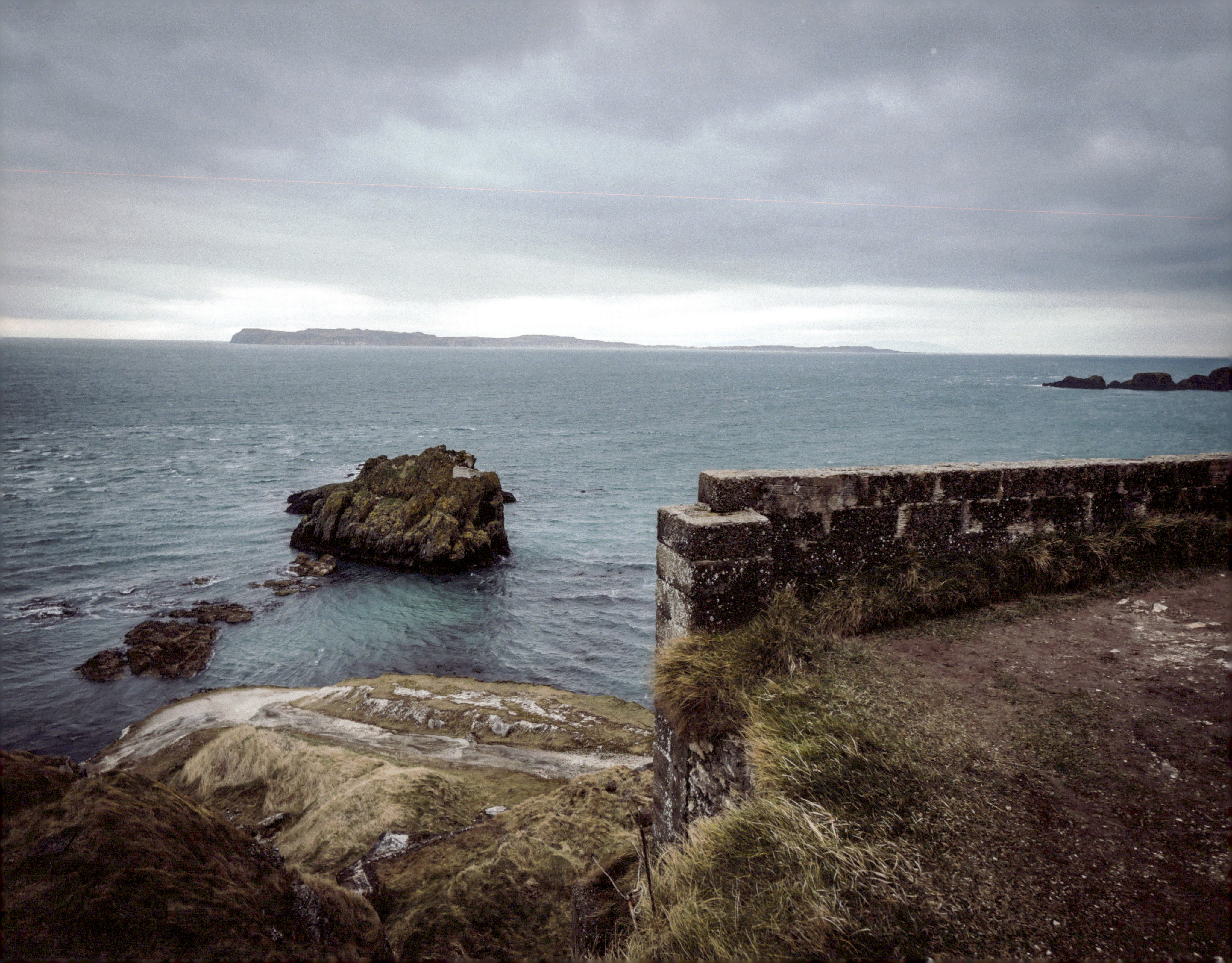

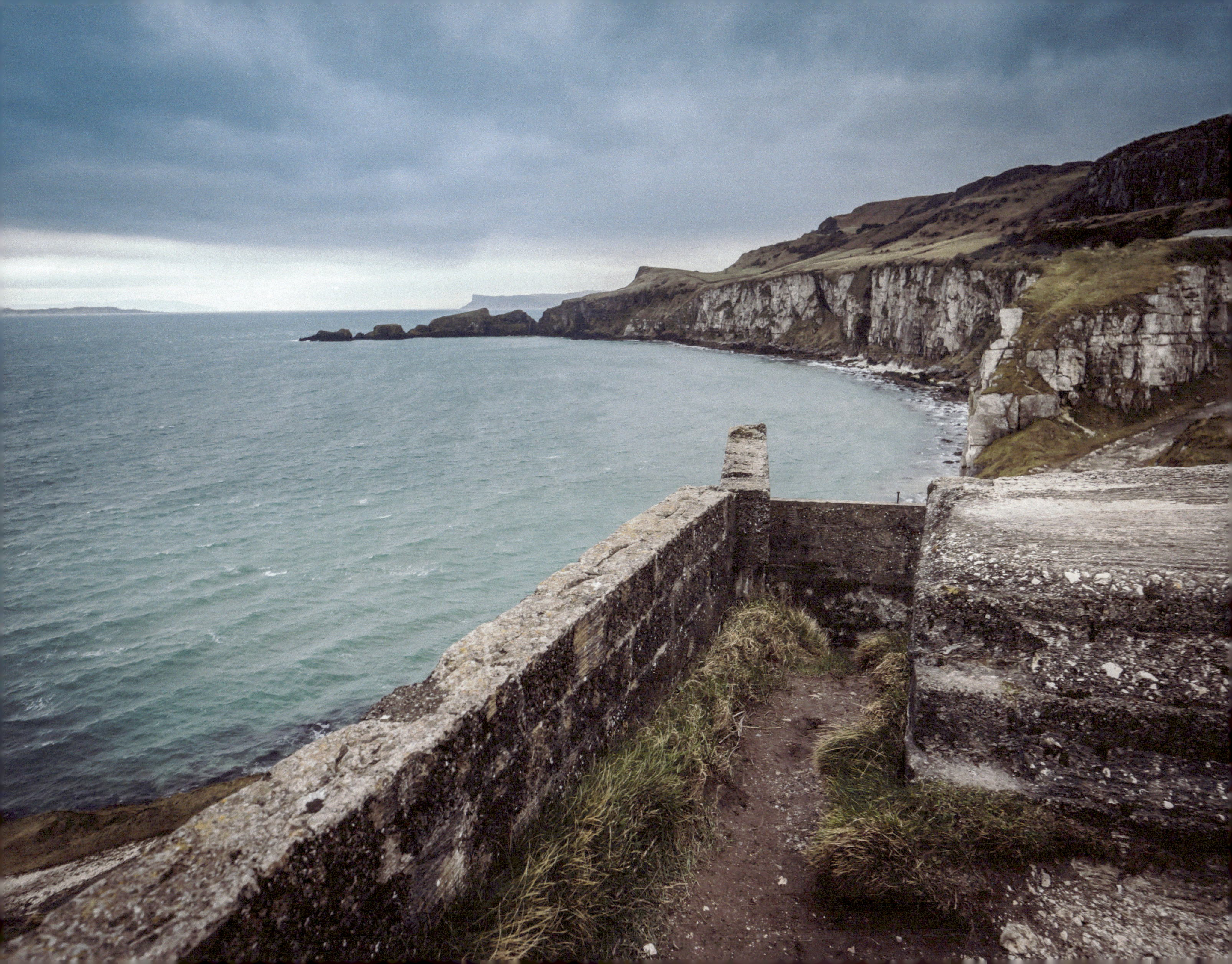

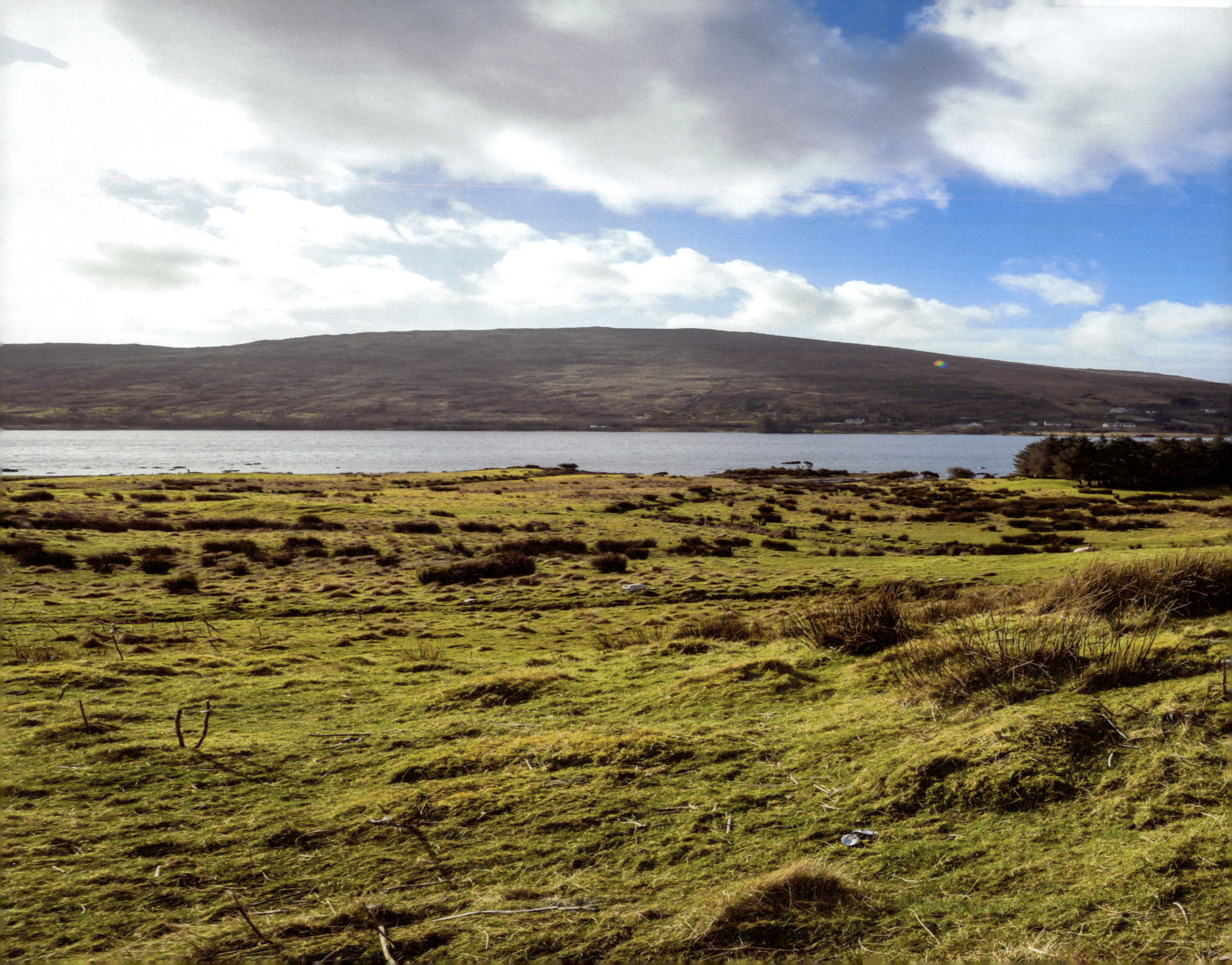

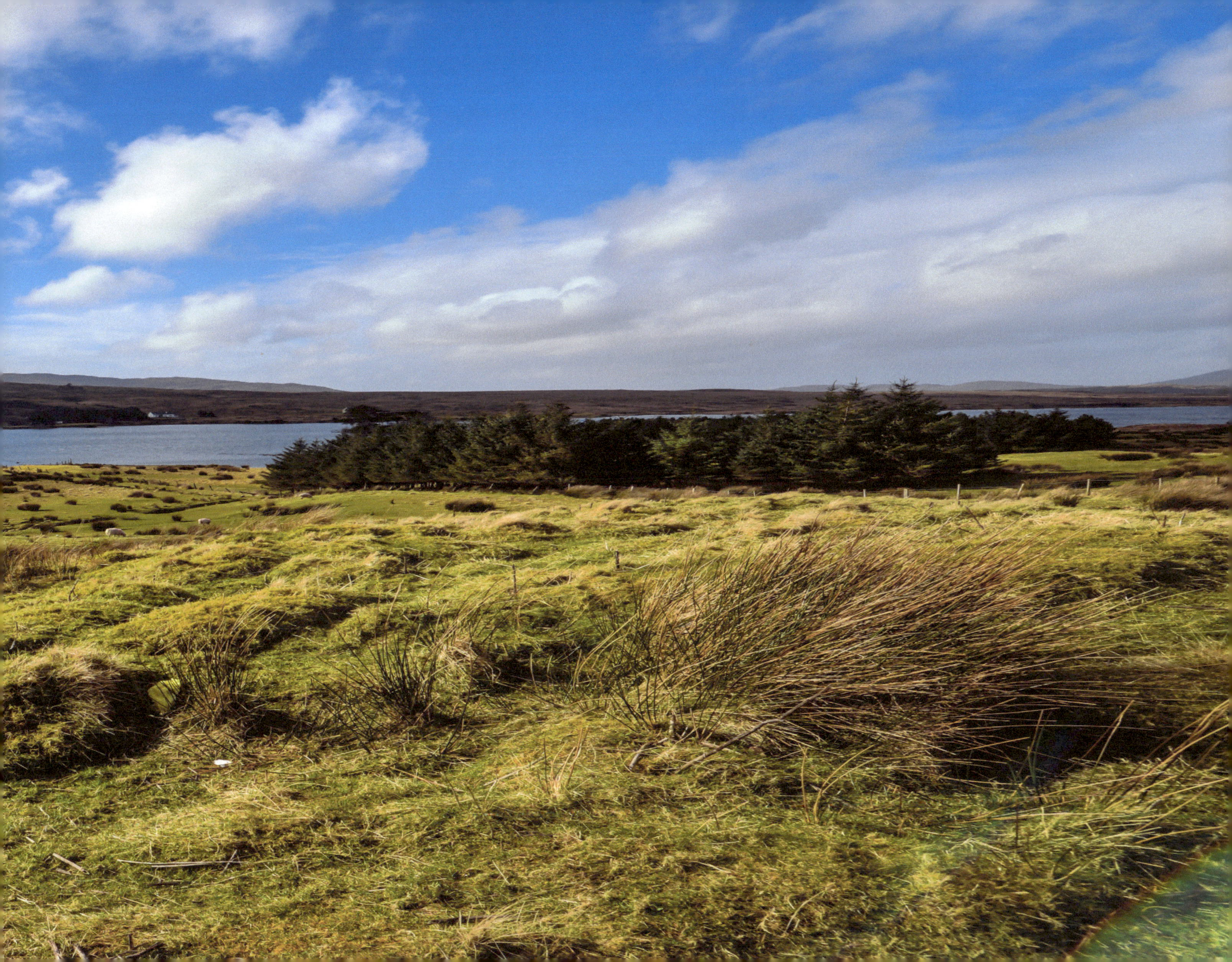

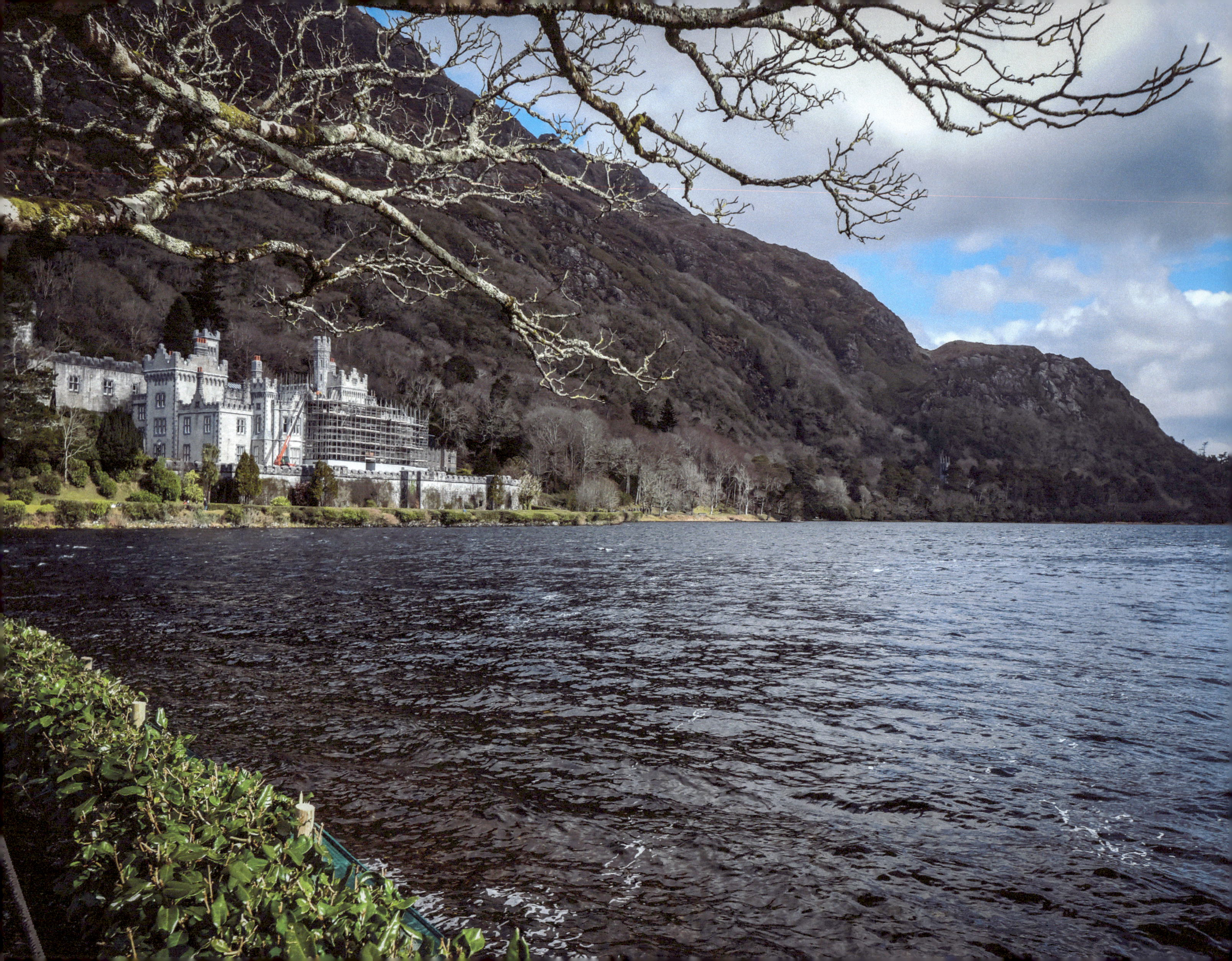

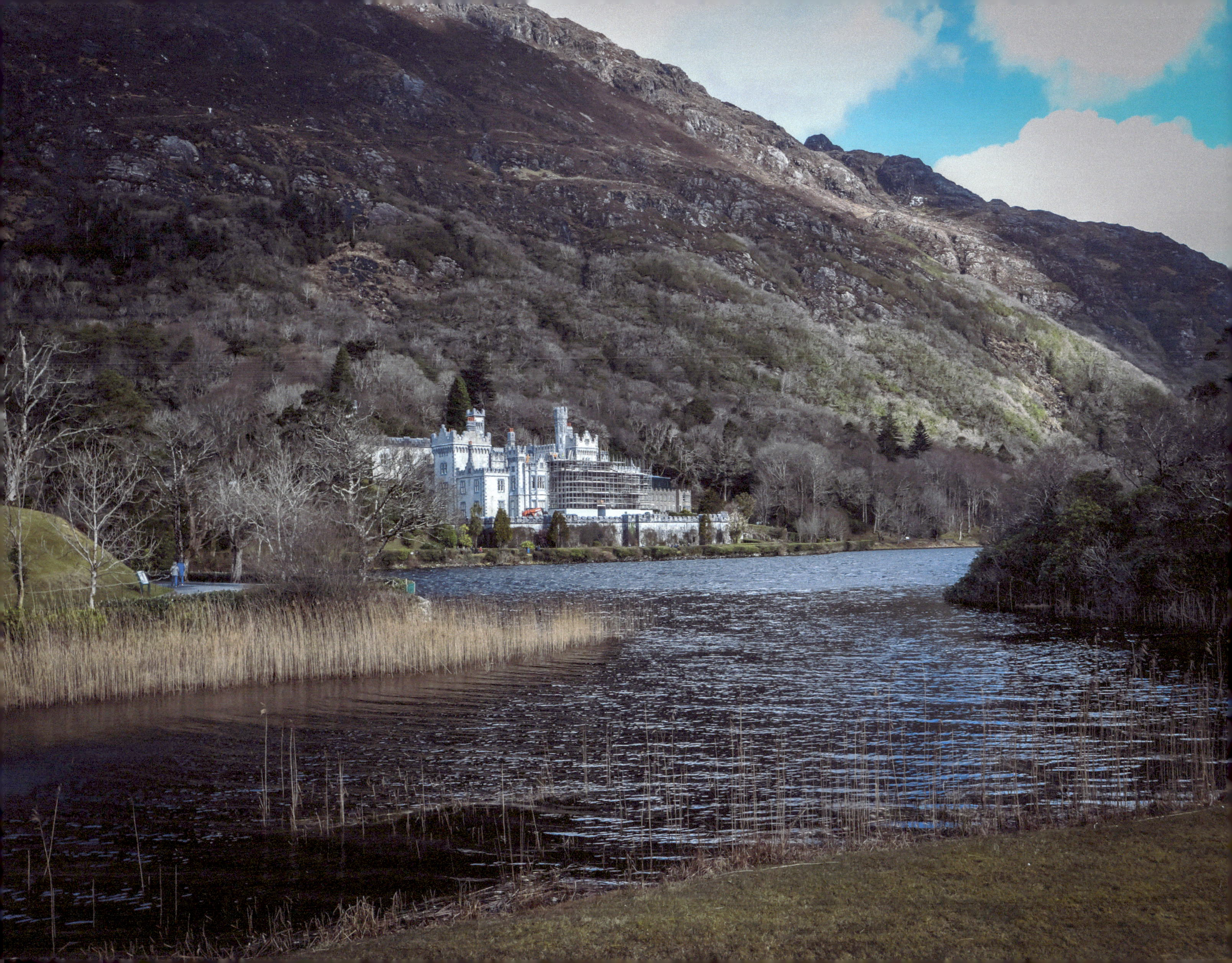

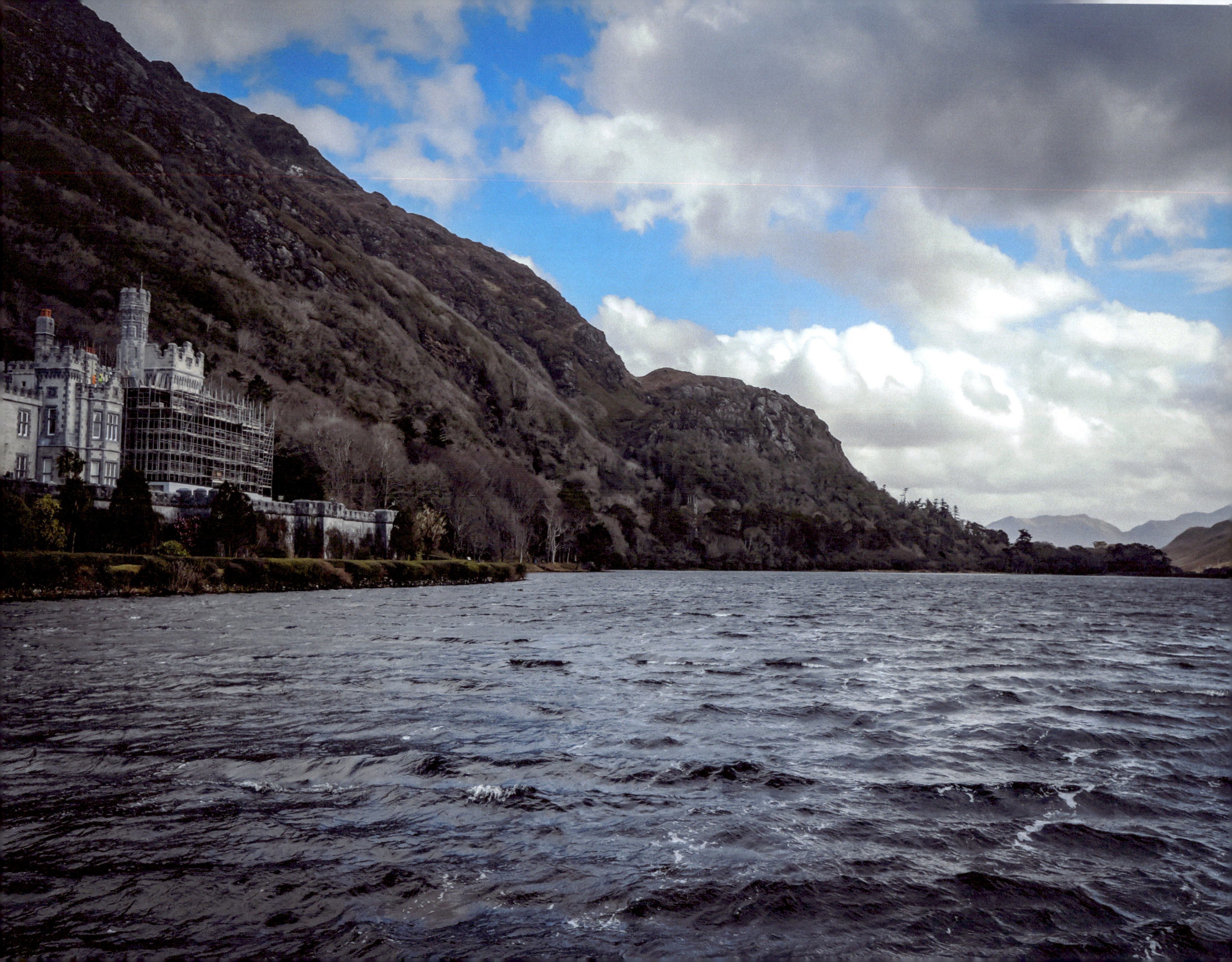

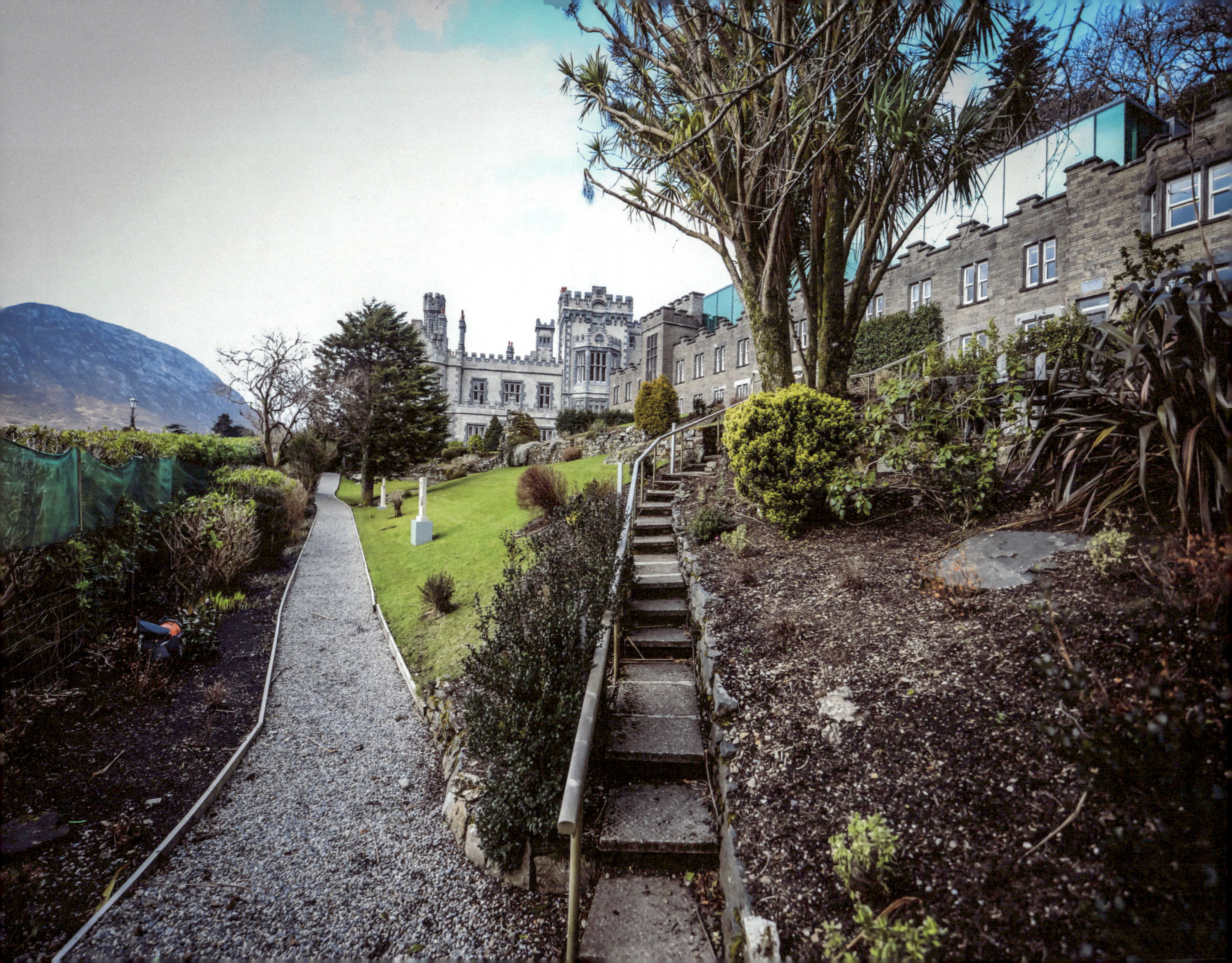

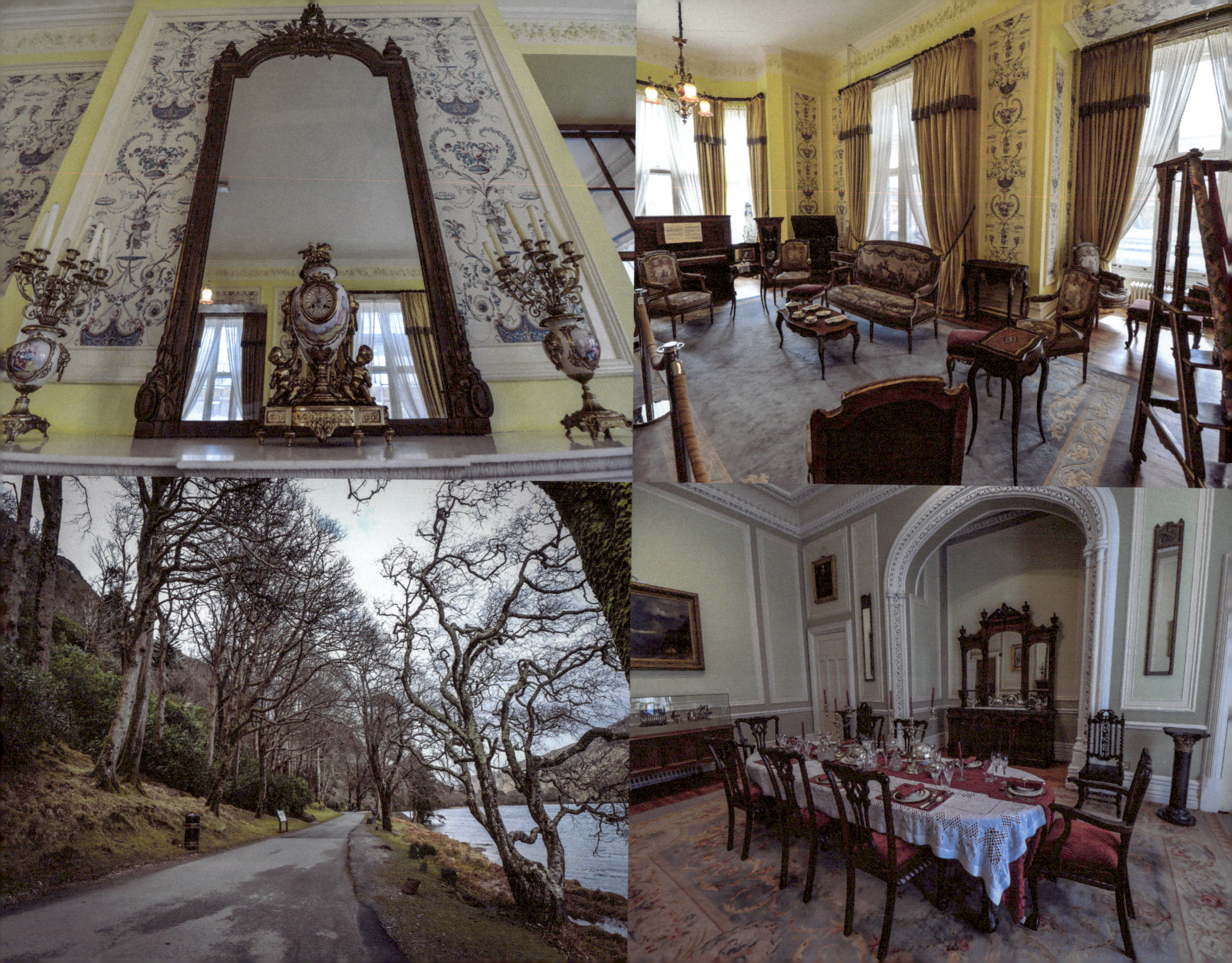

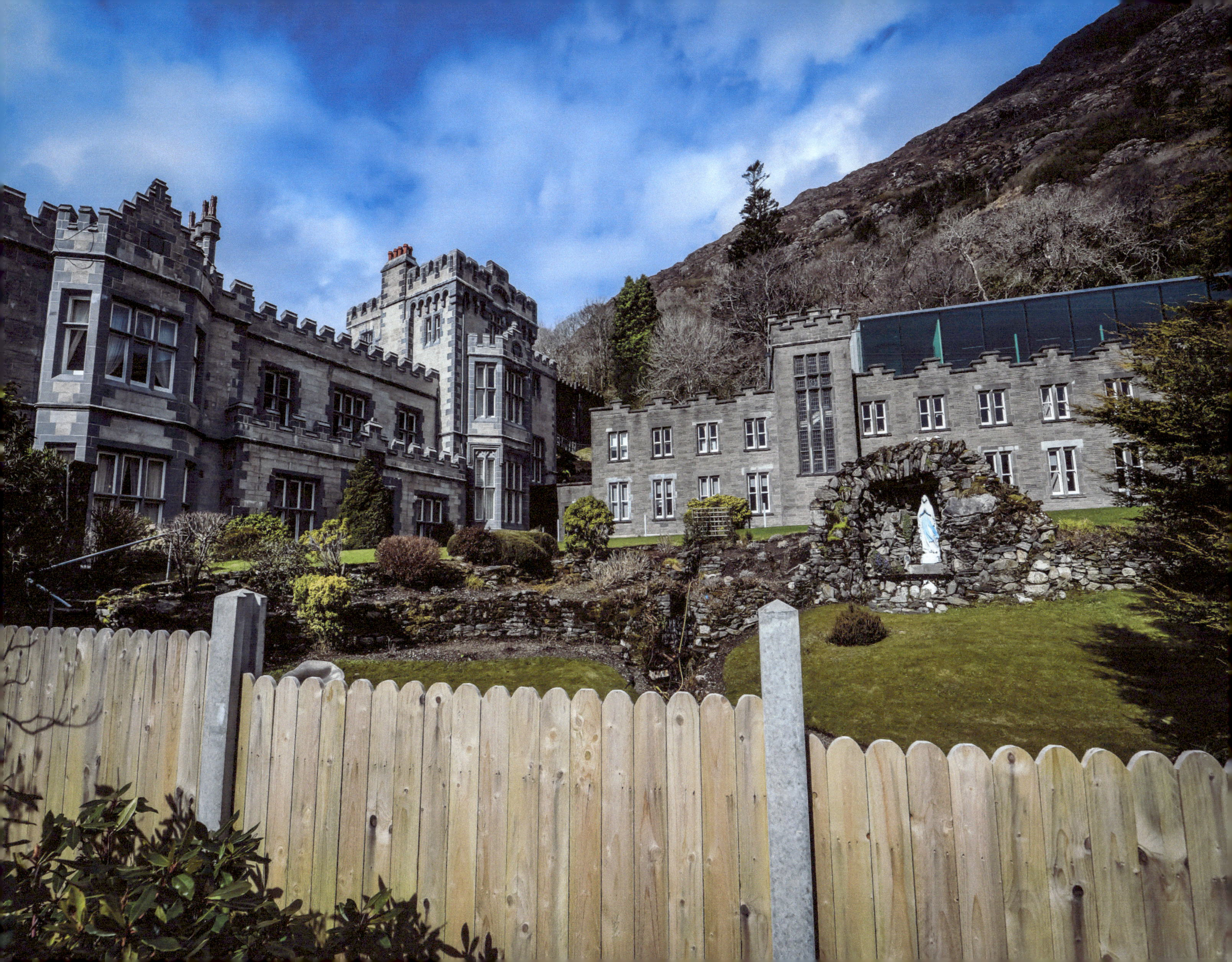

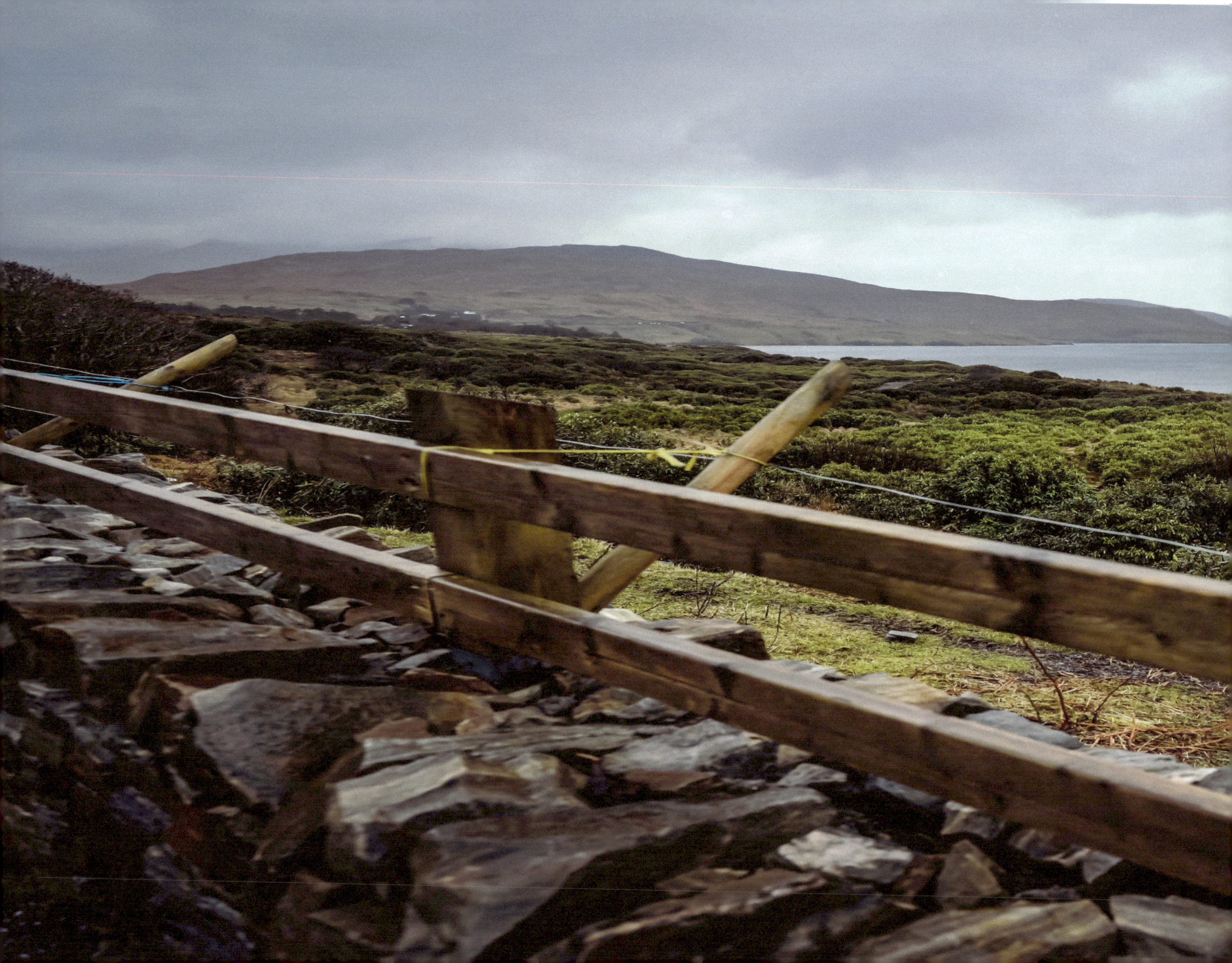

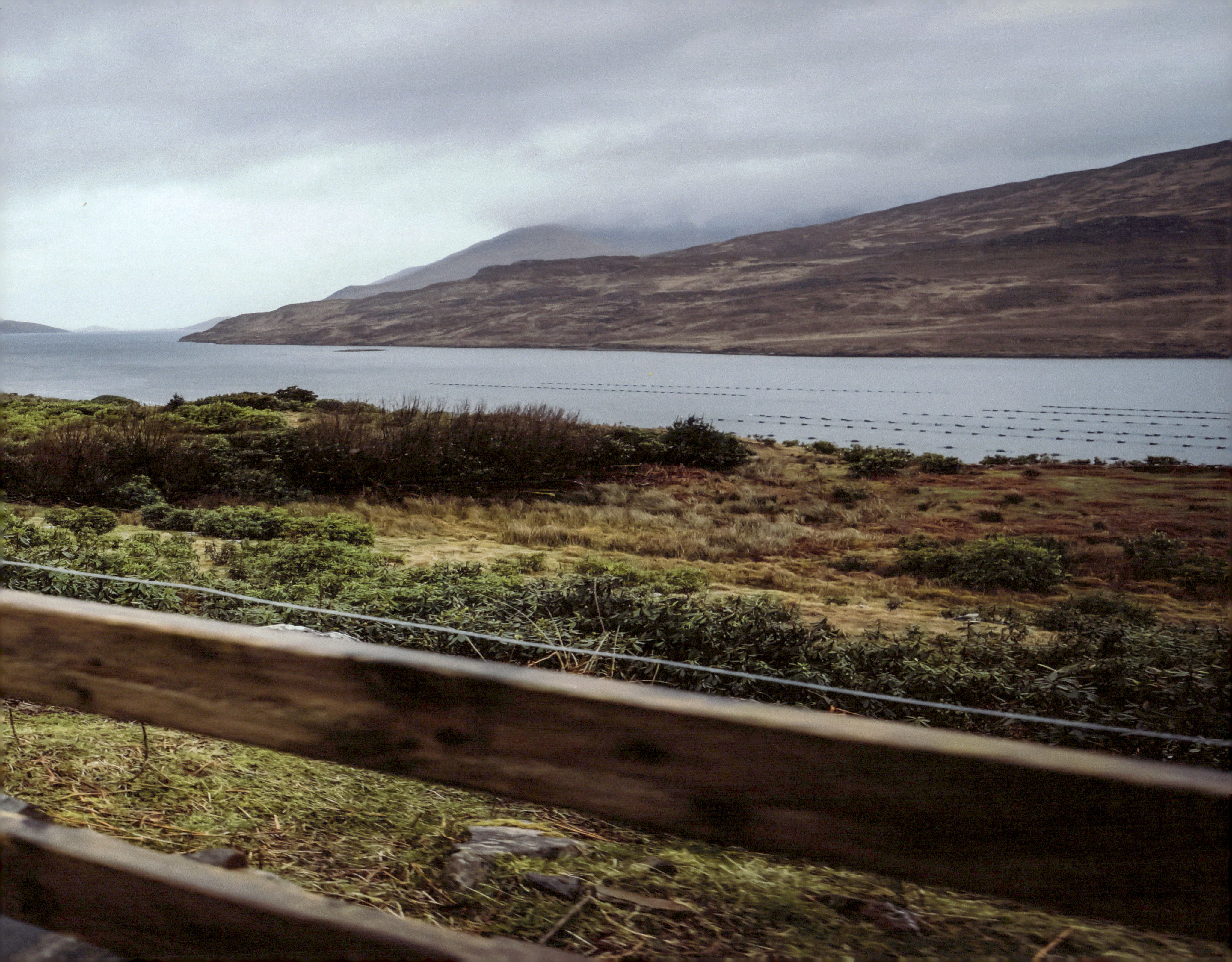

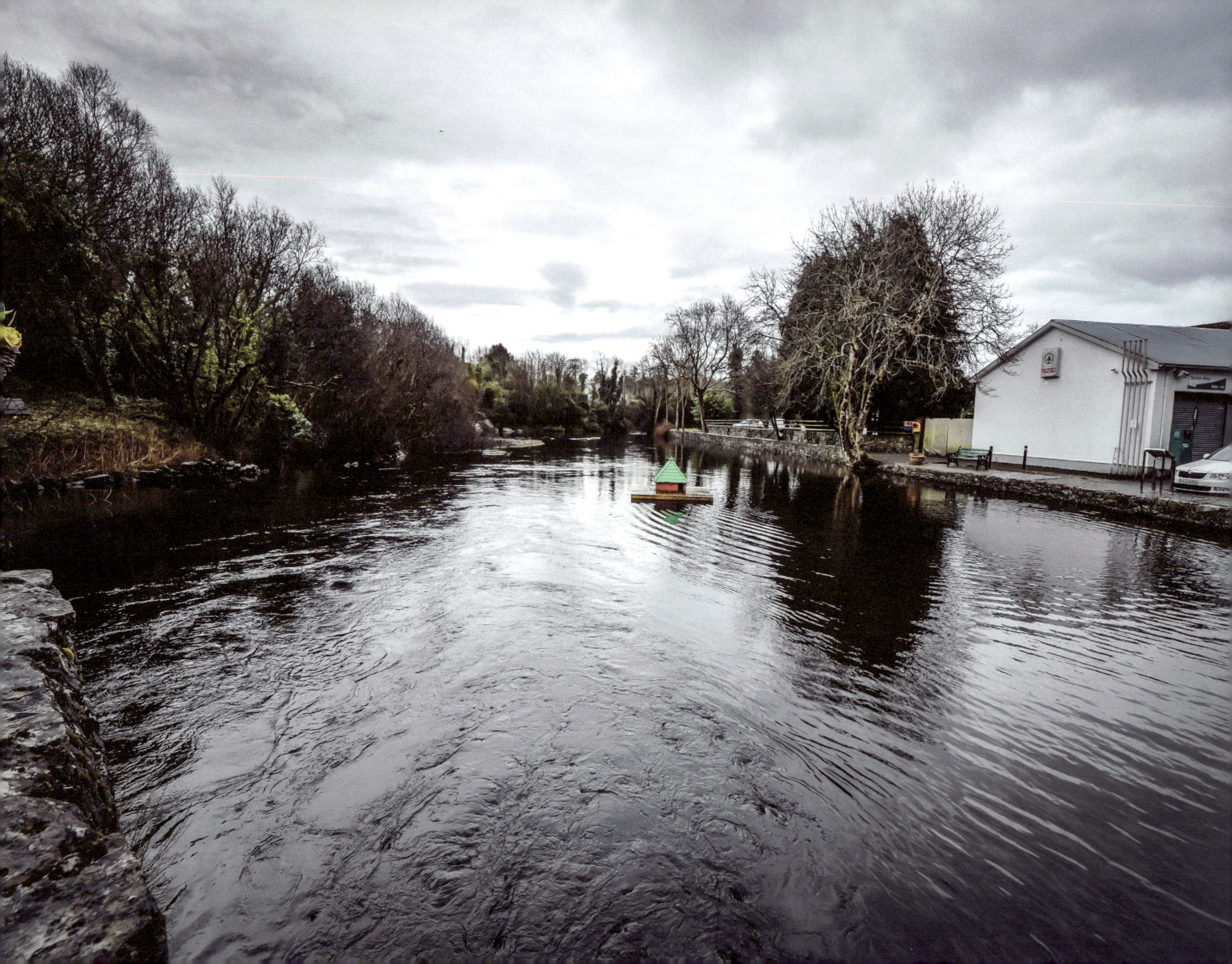

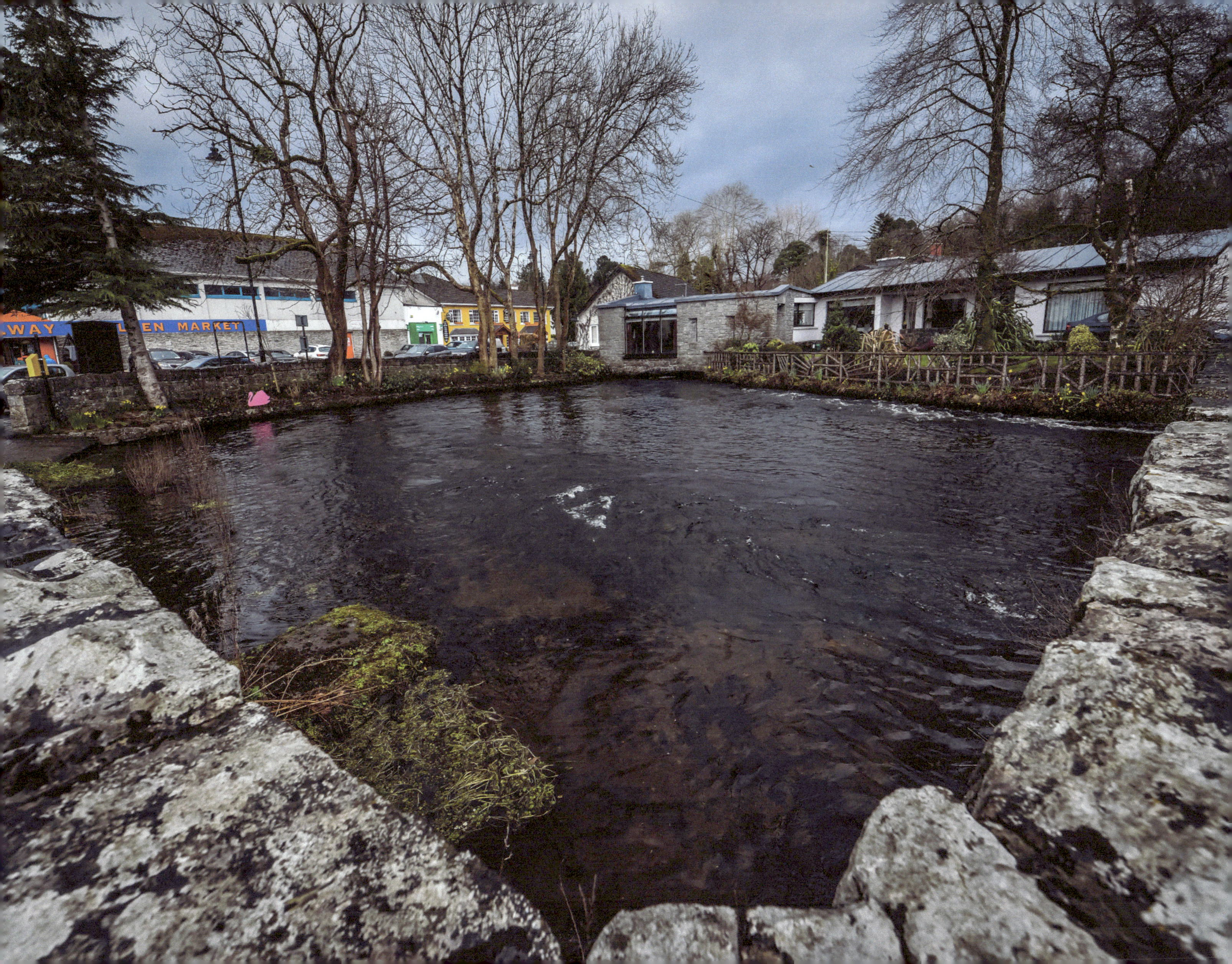
WAY
EN MARKET

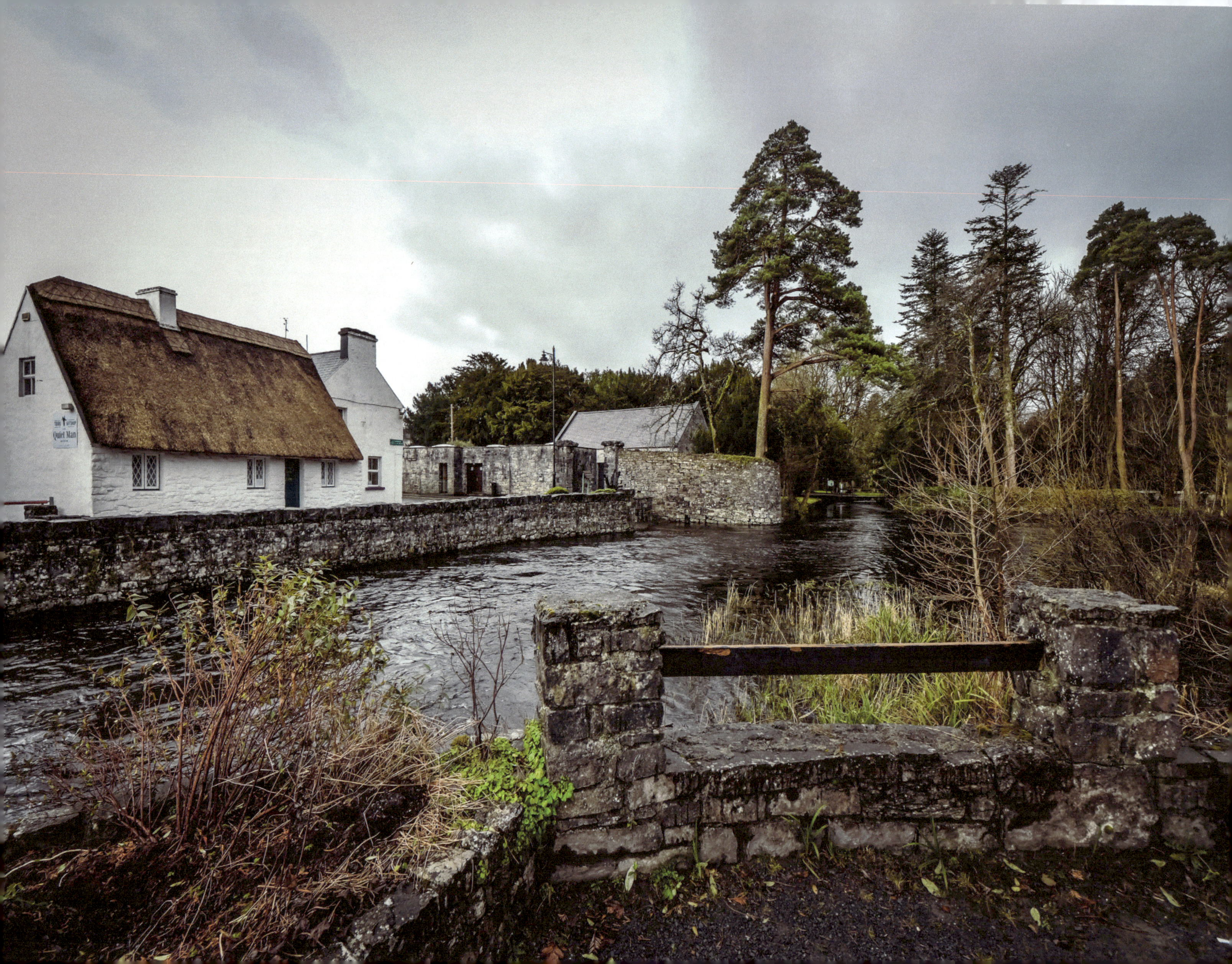

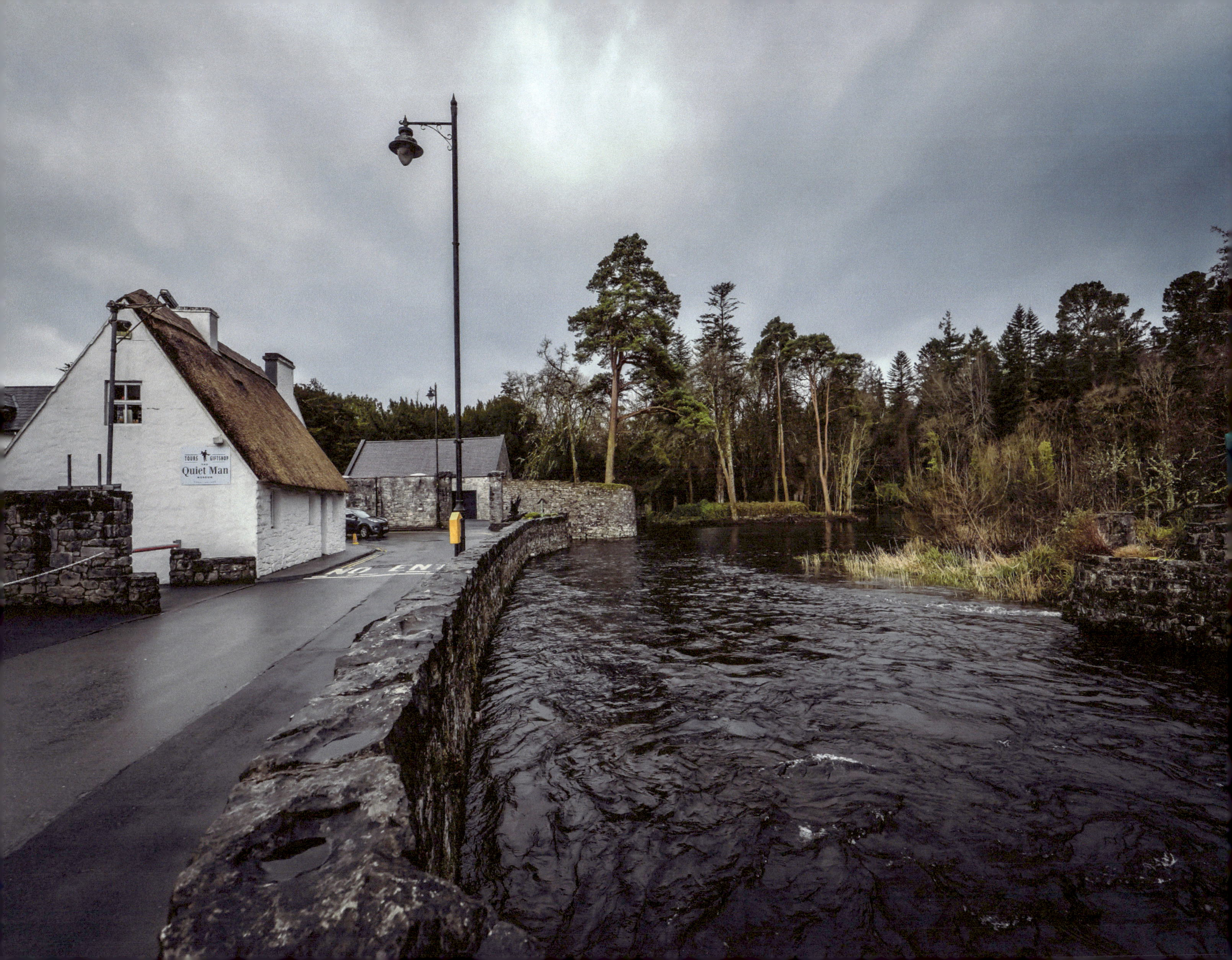

TOURS   GIFTSHOP
THE
Quiet Man
MUSEUM

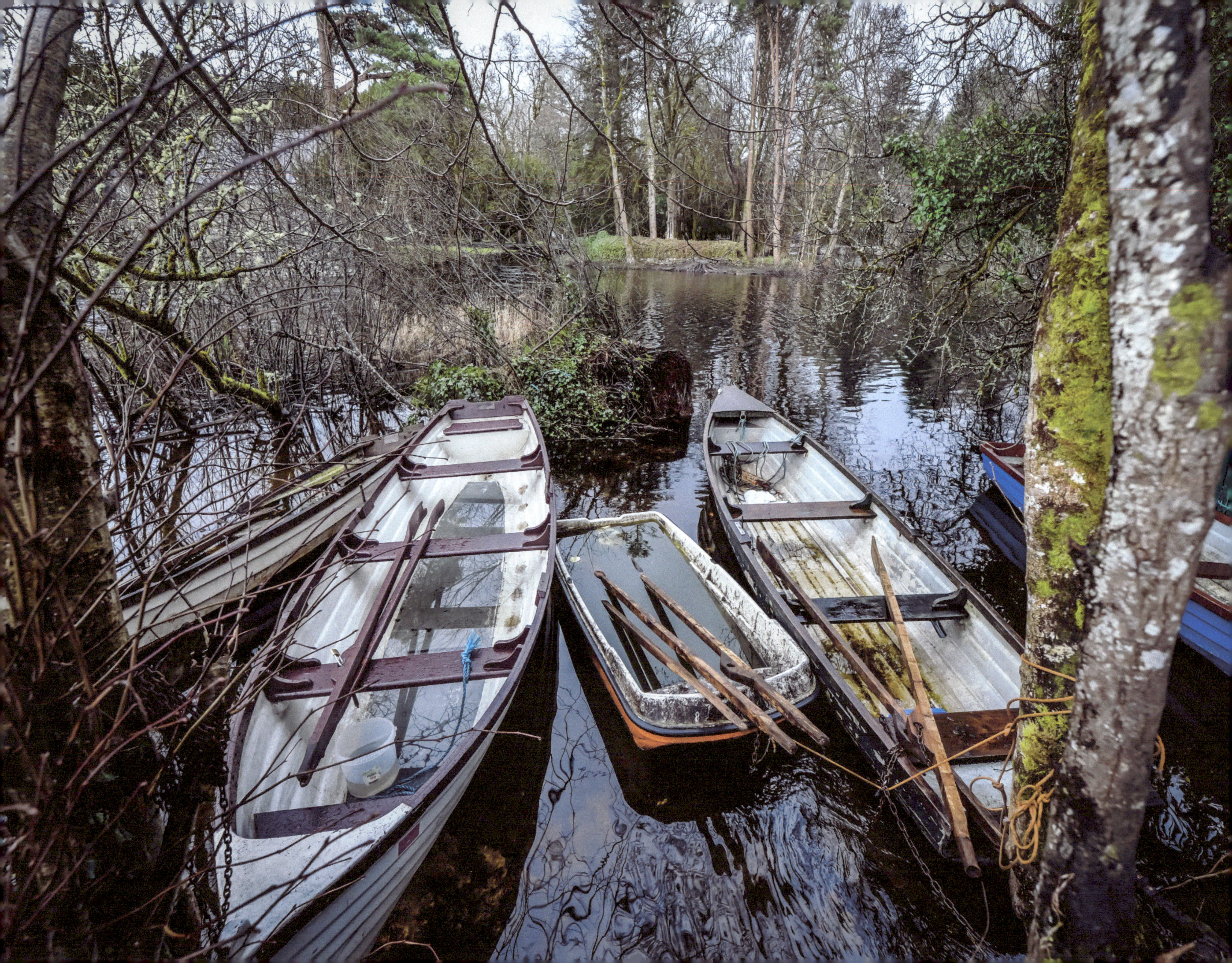

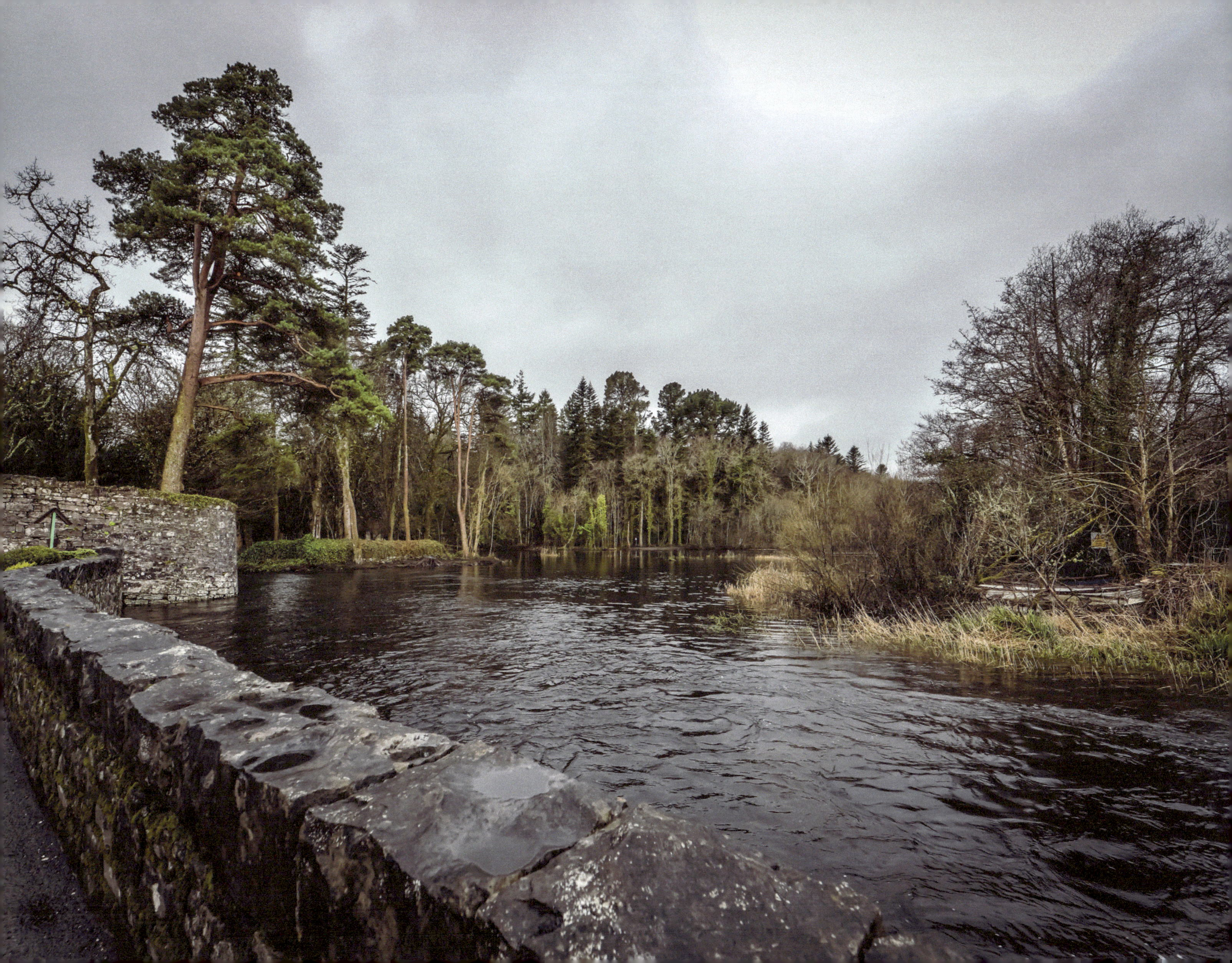

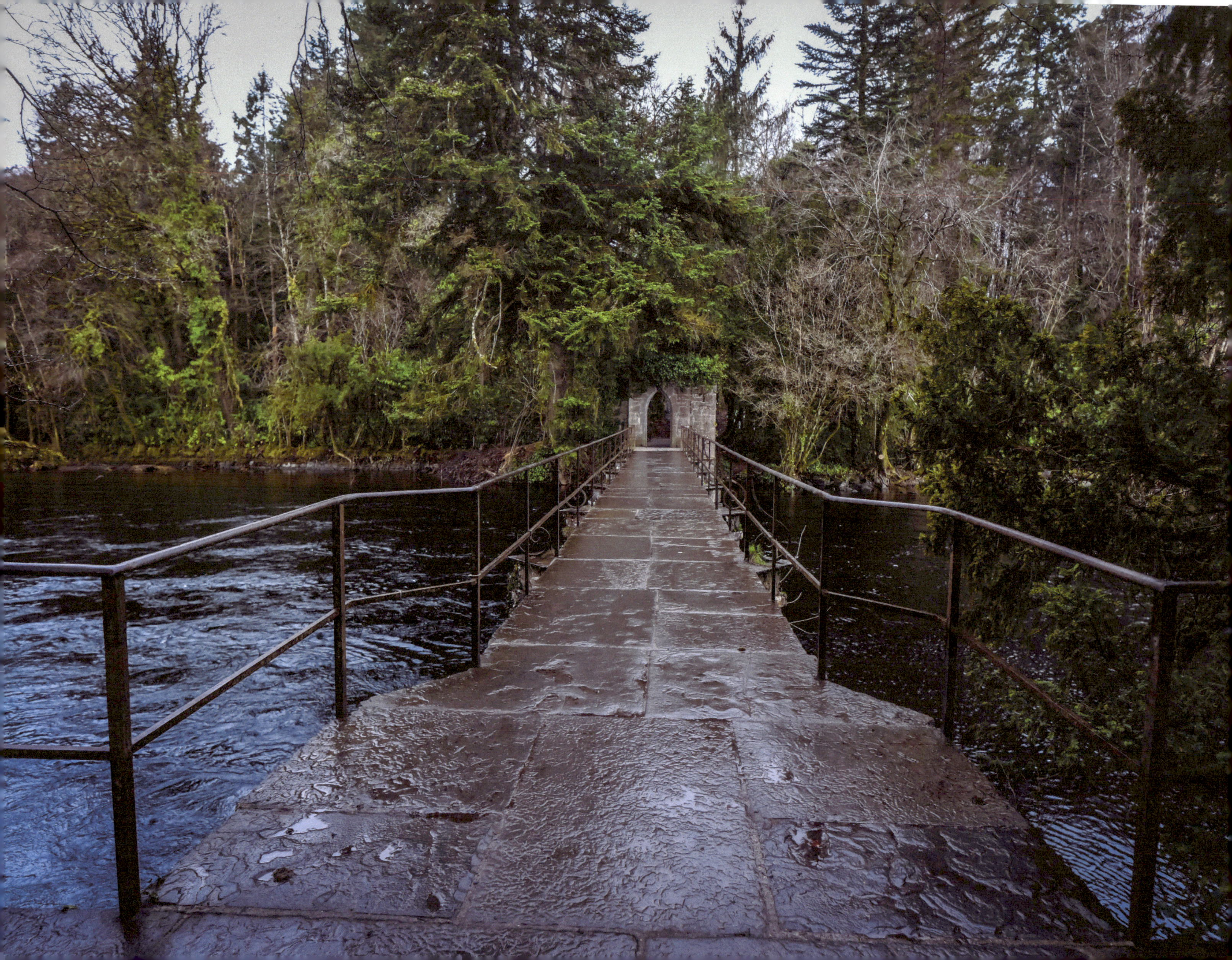

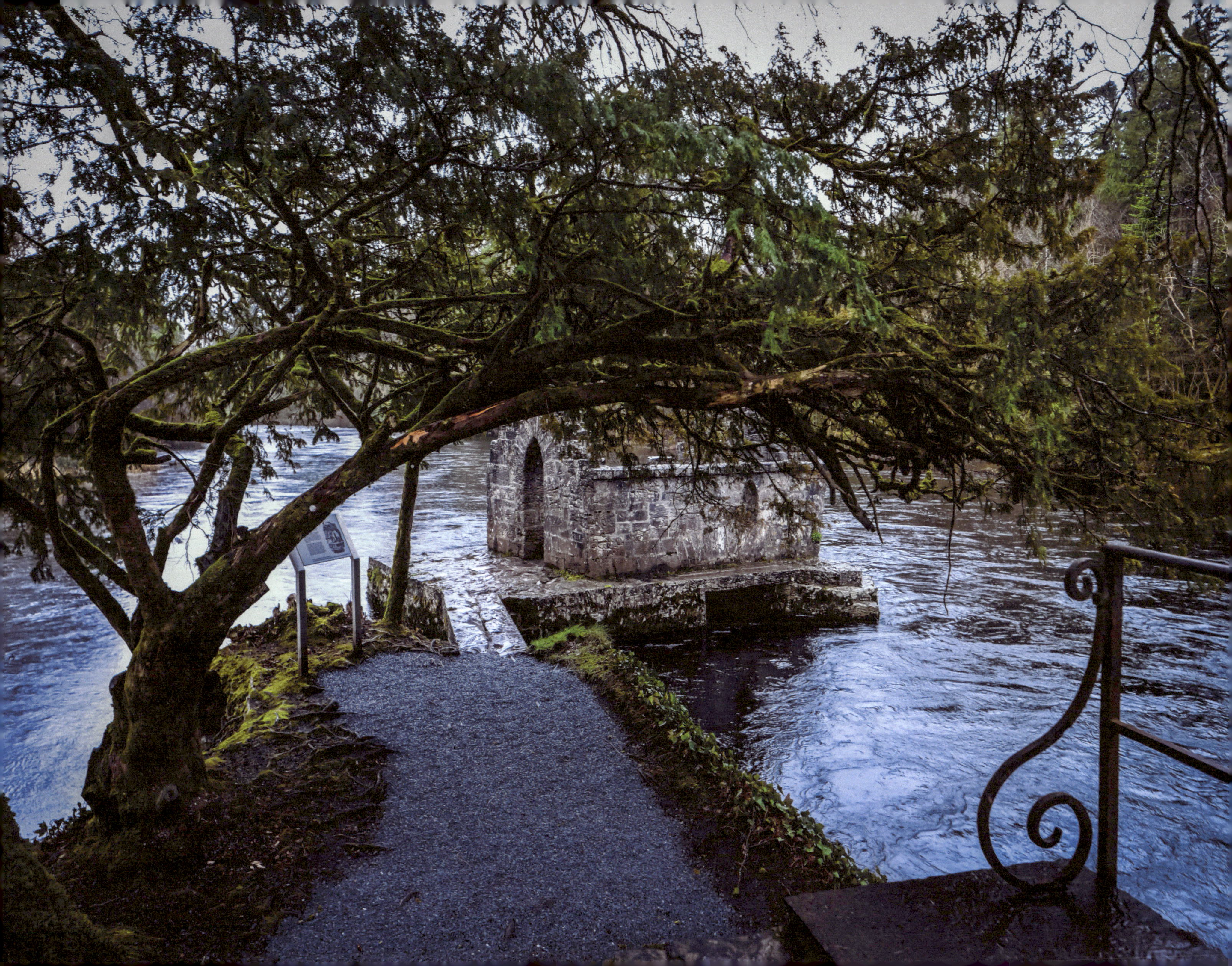

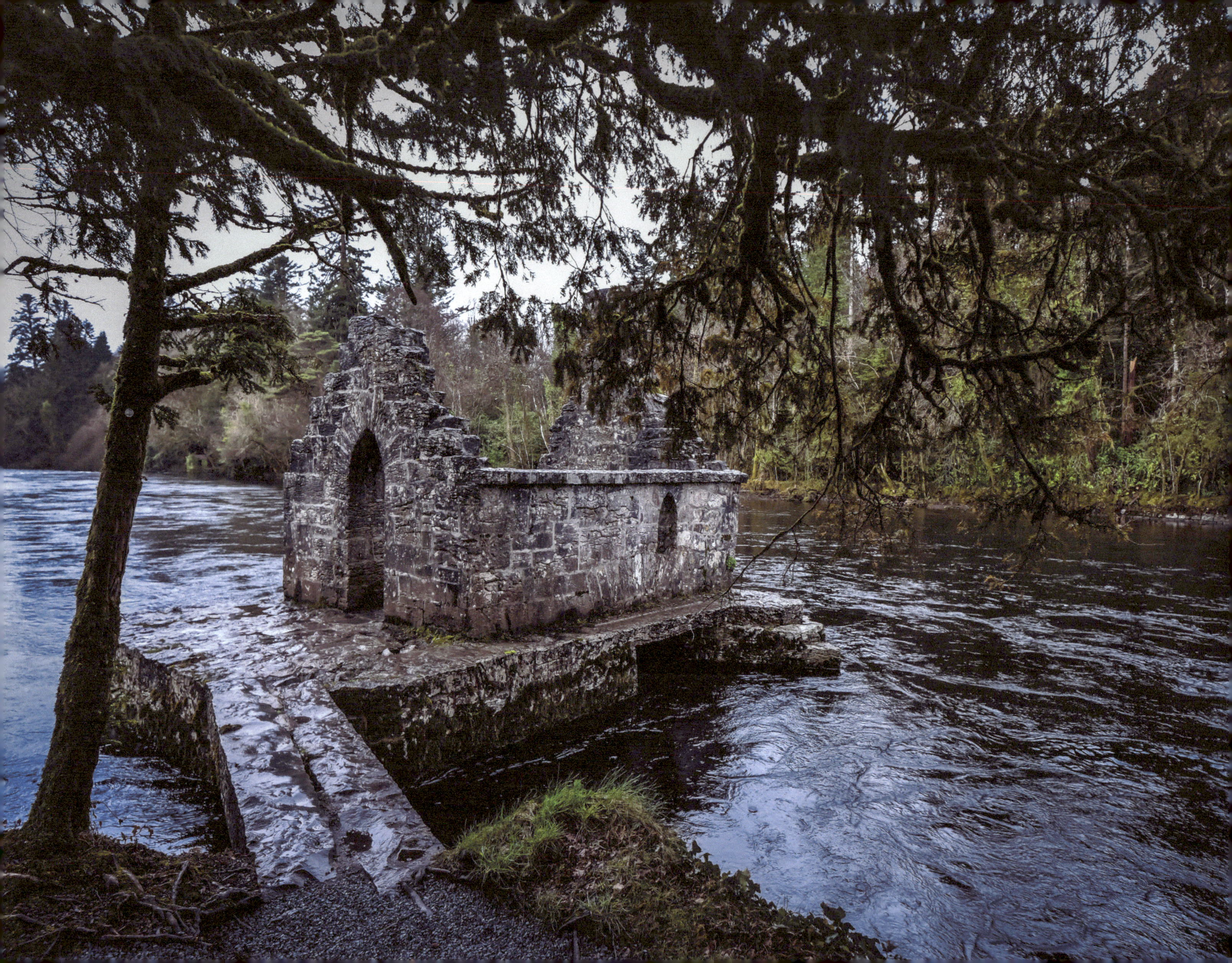

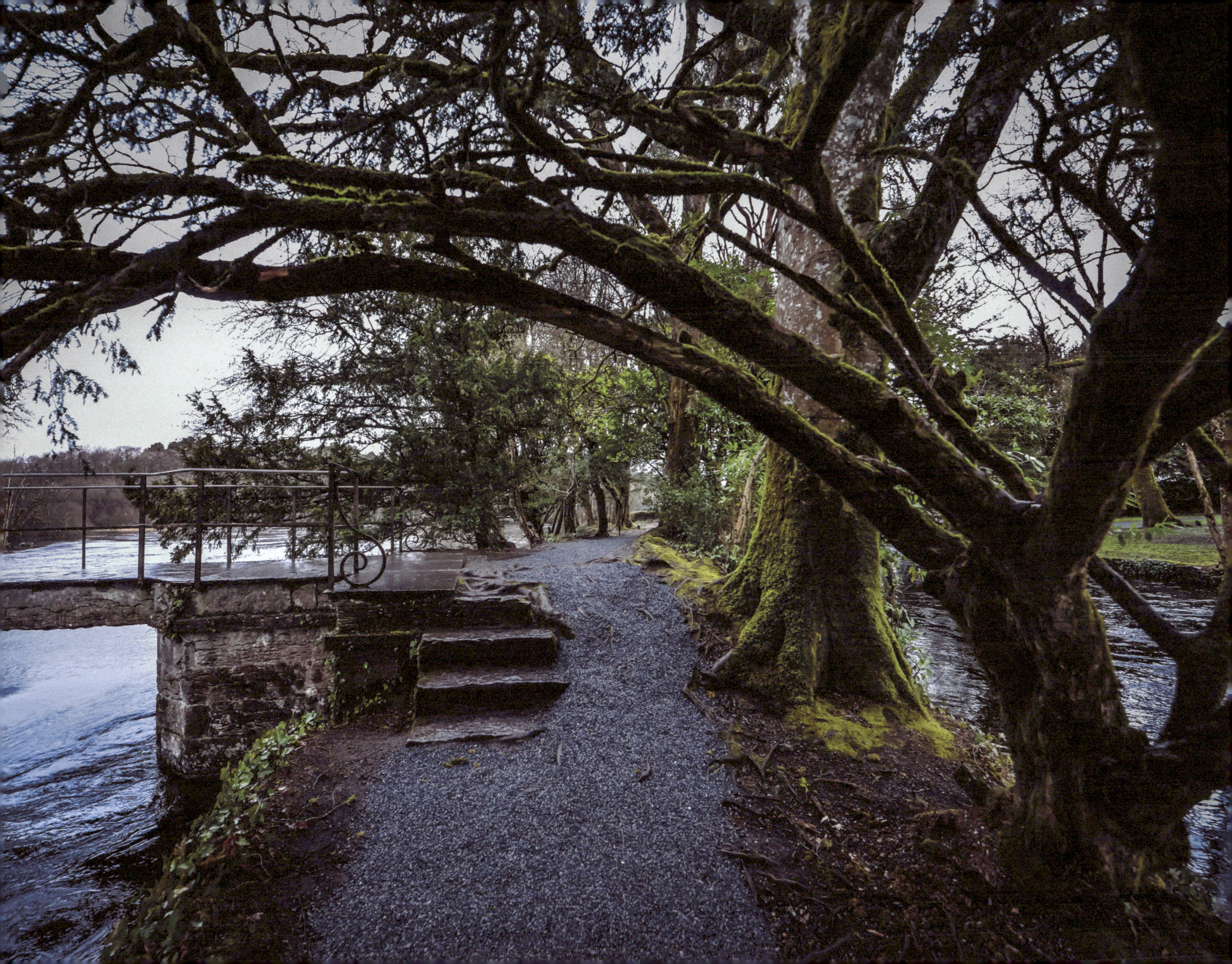

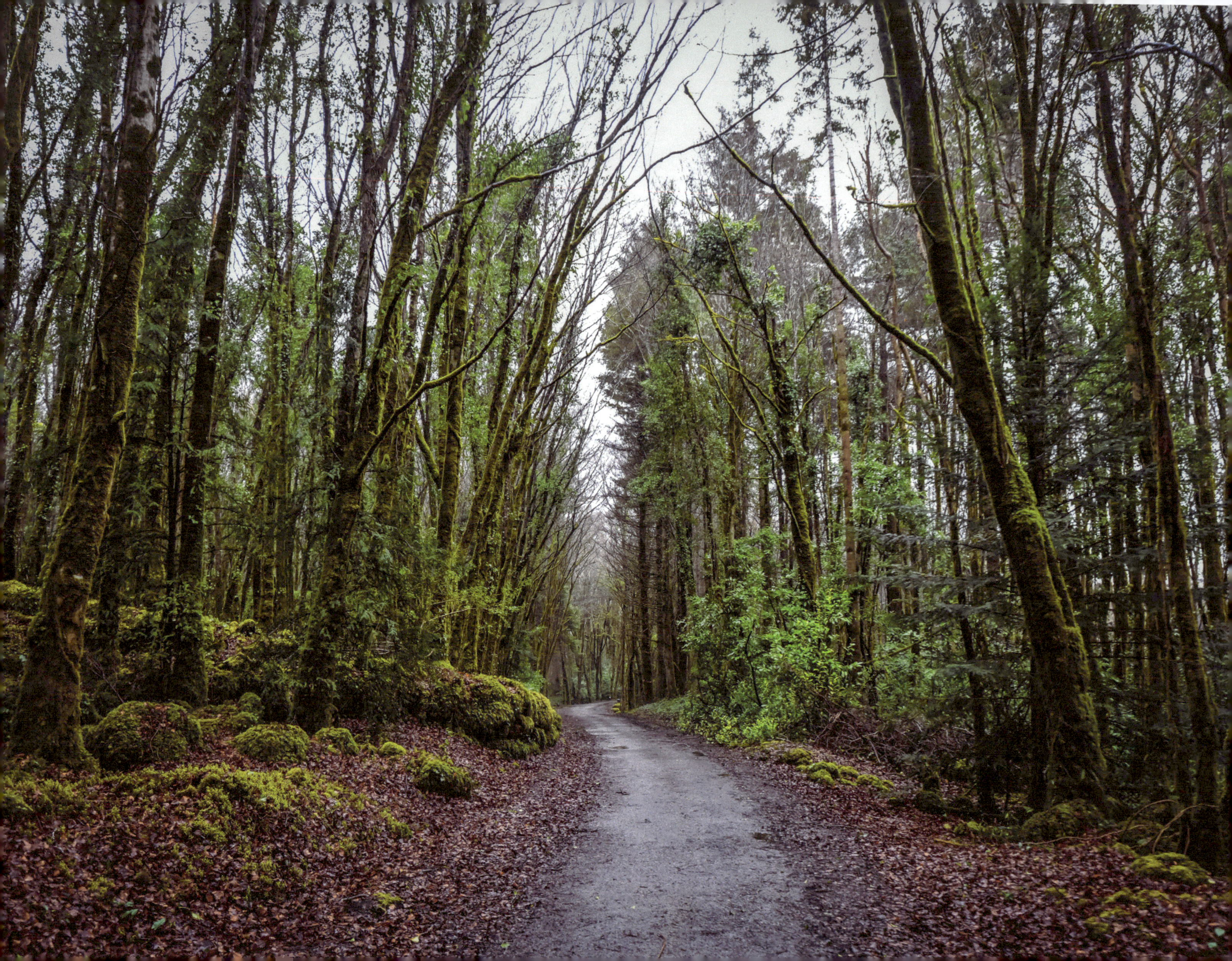

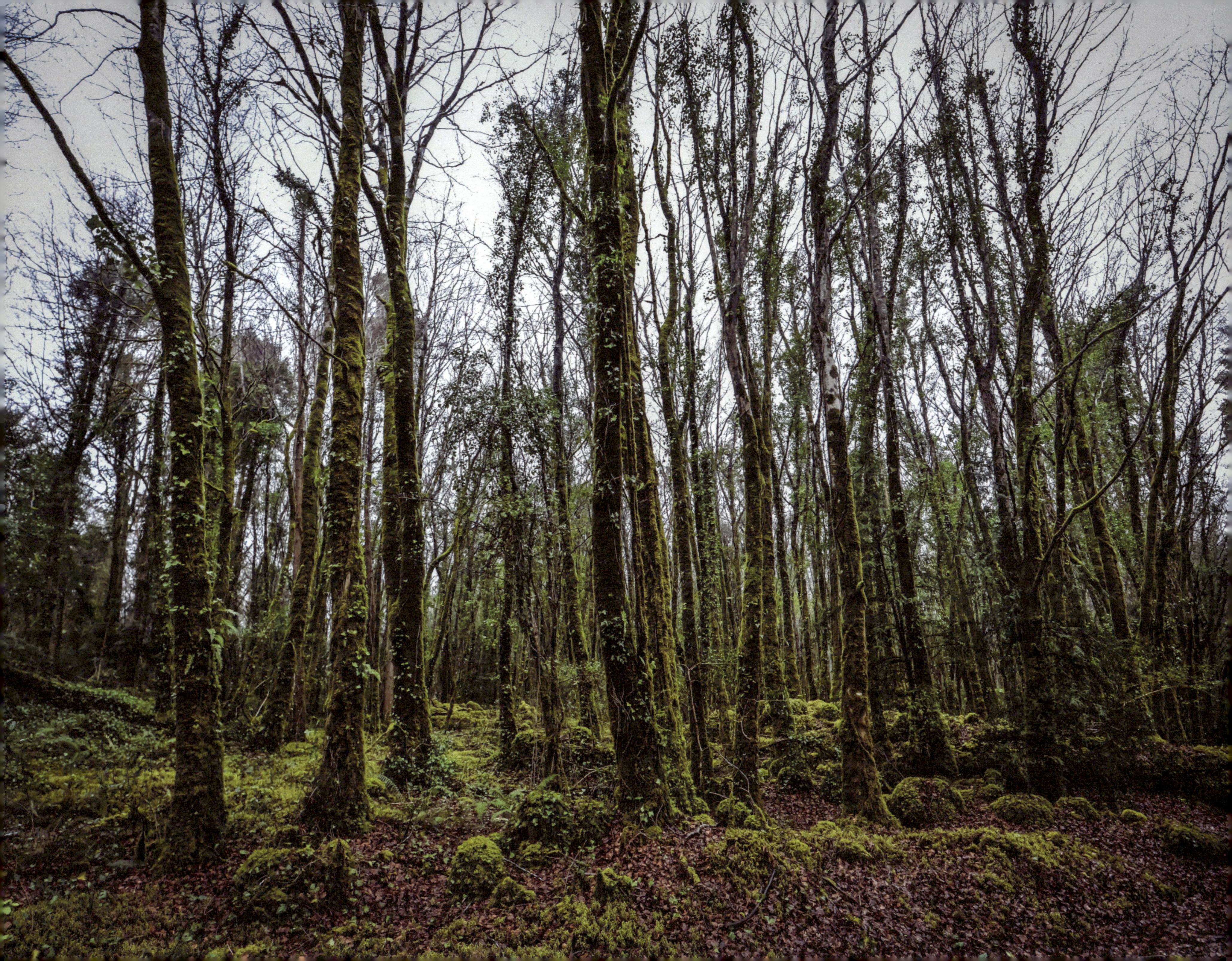

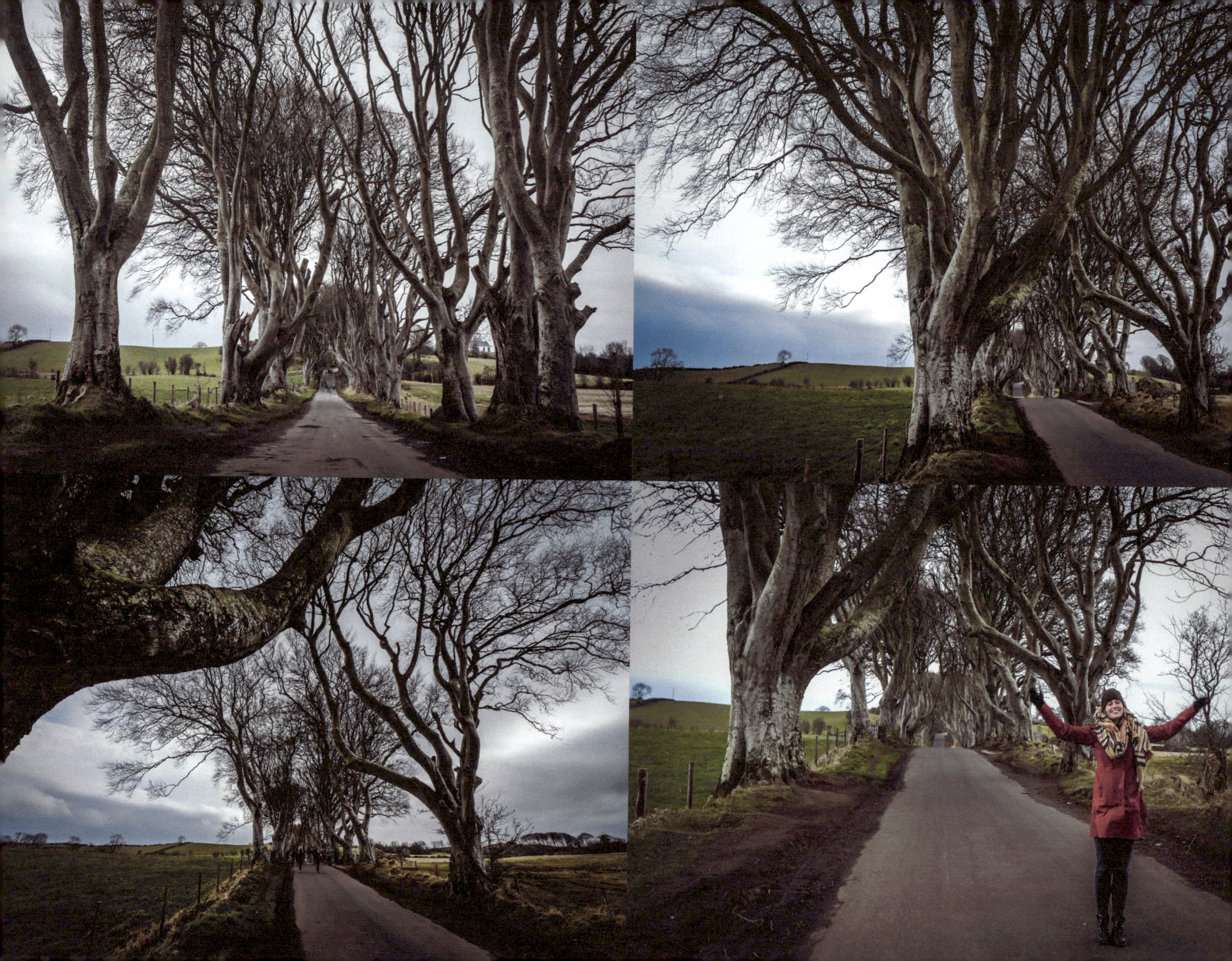

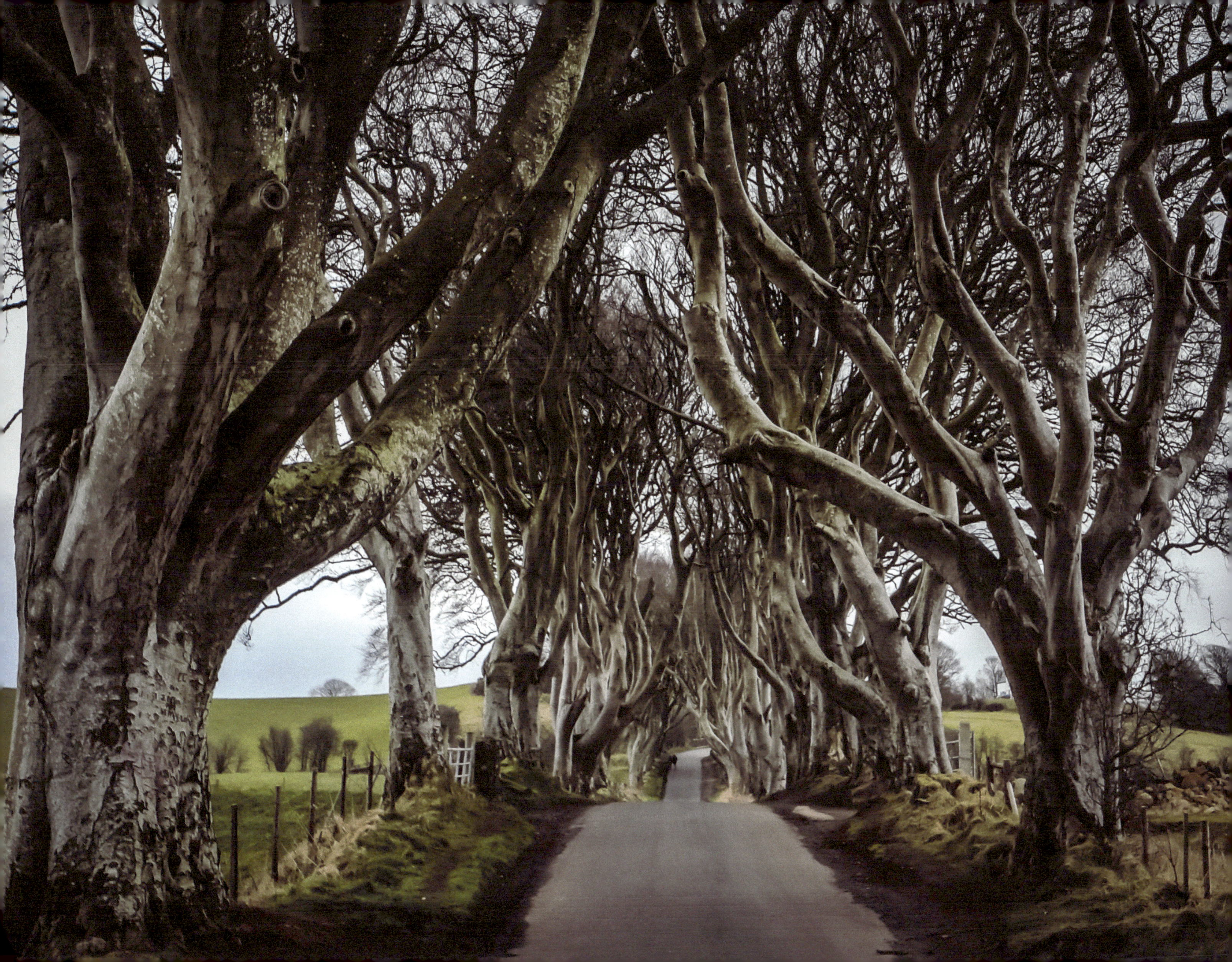

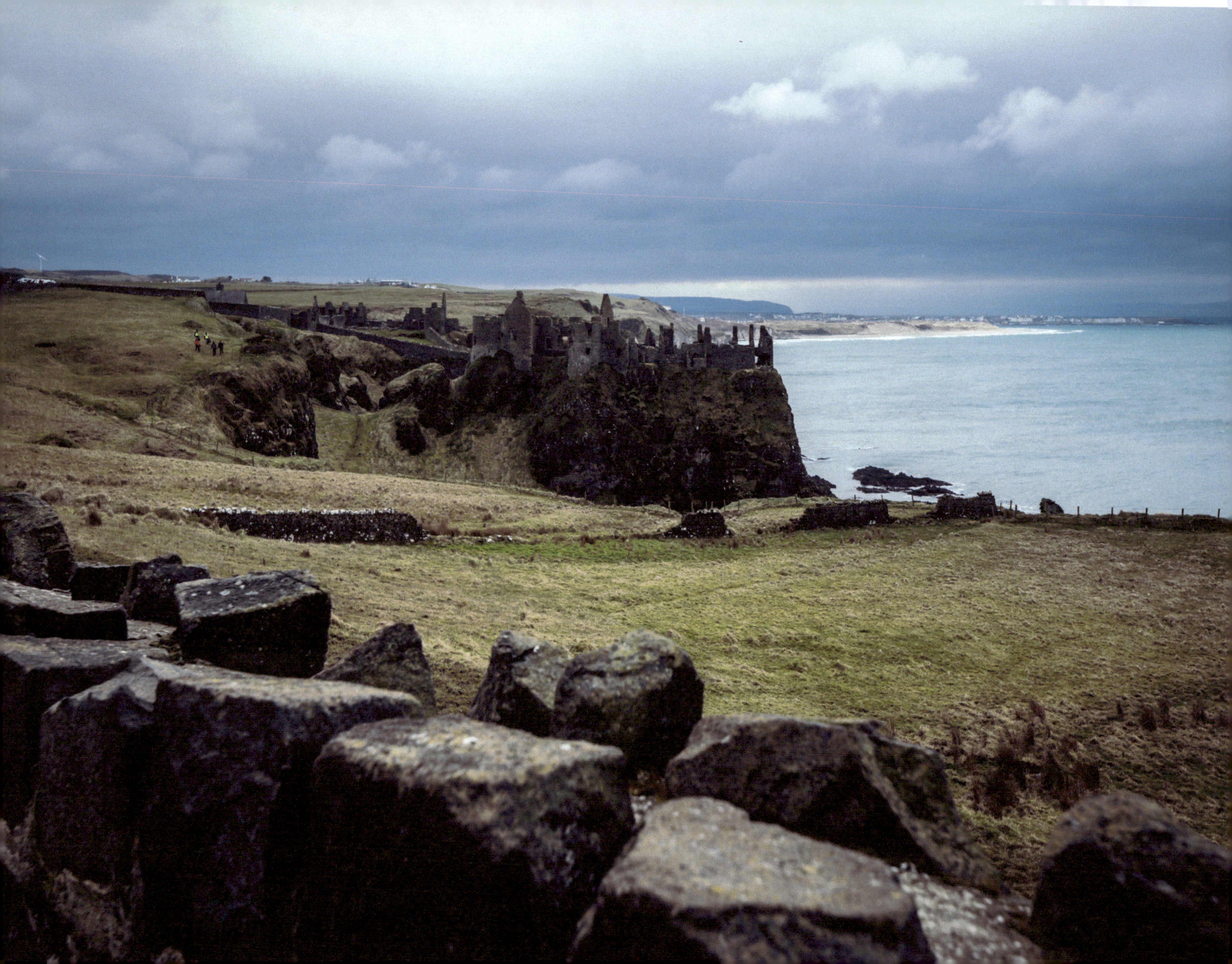

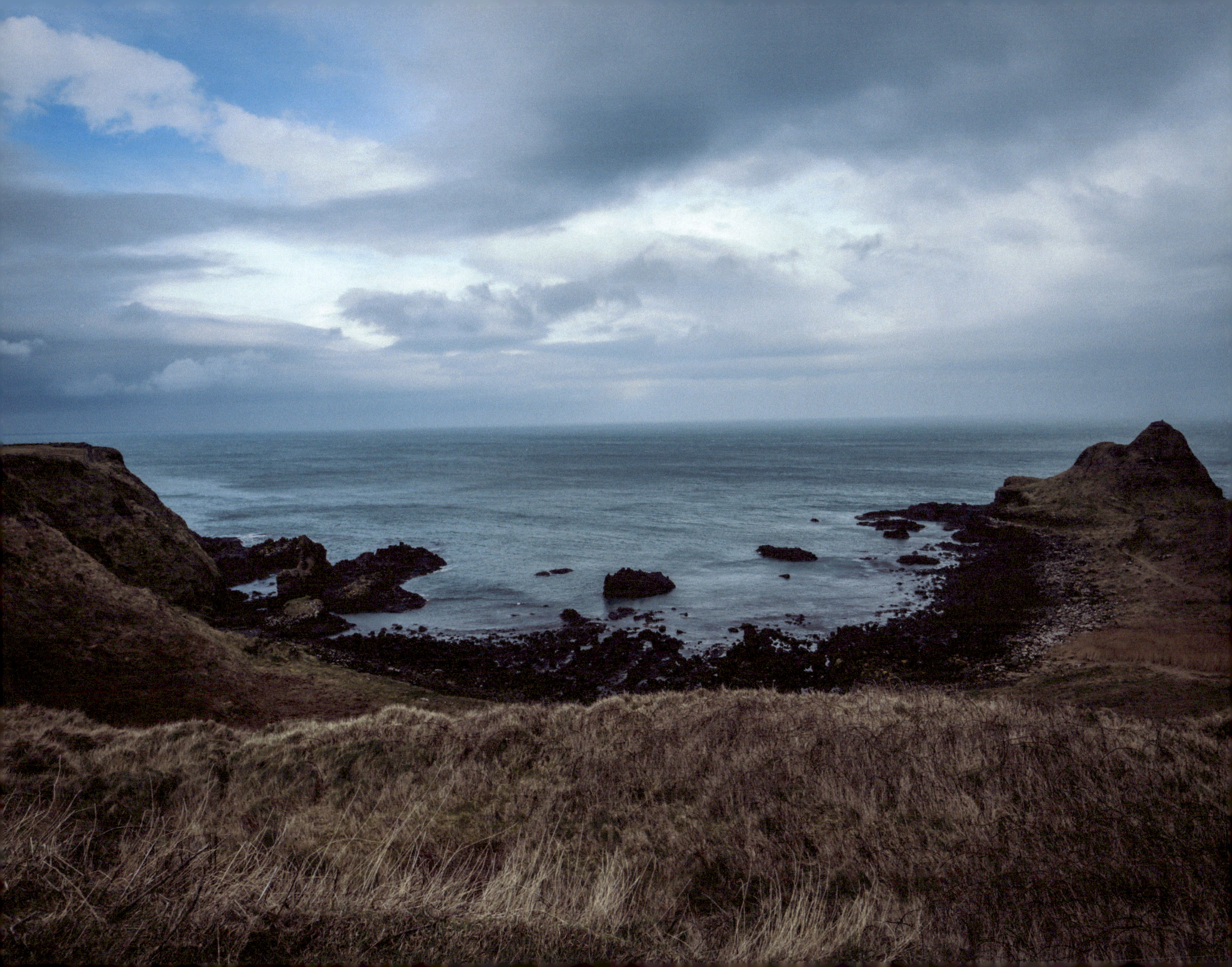

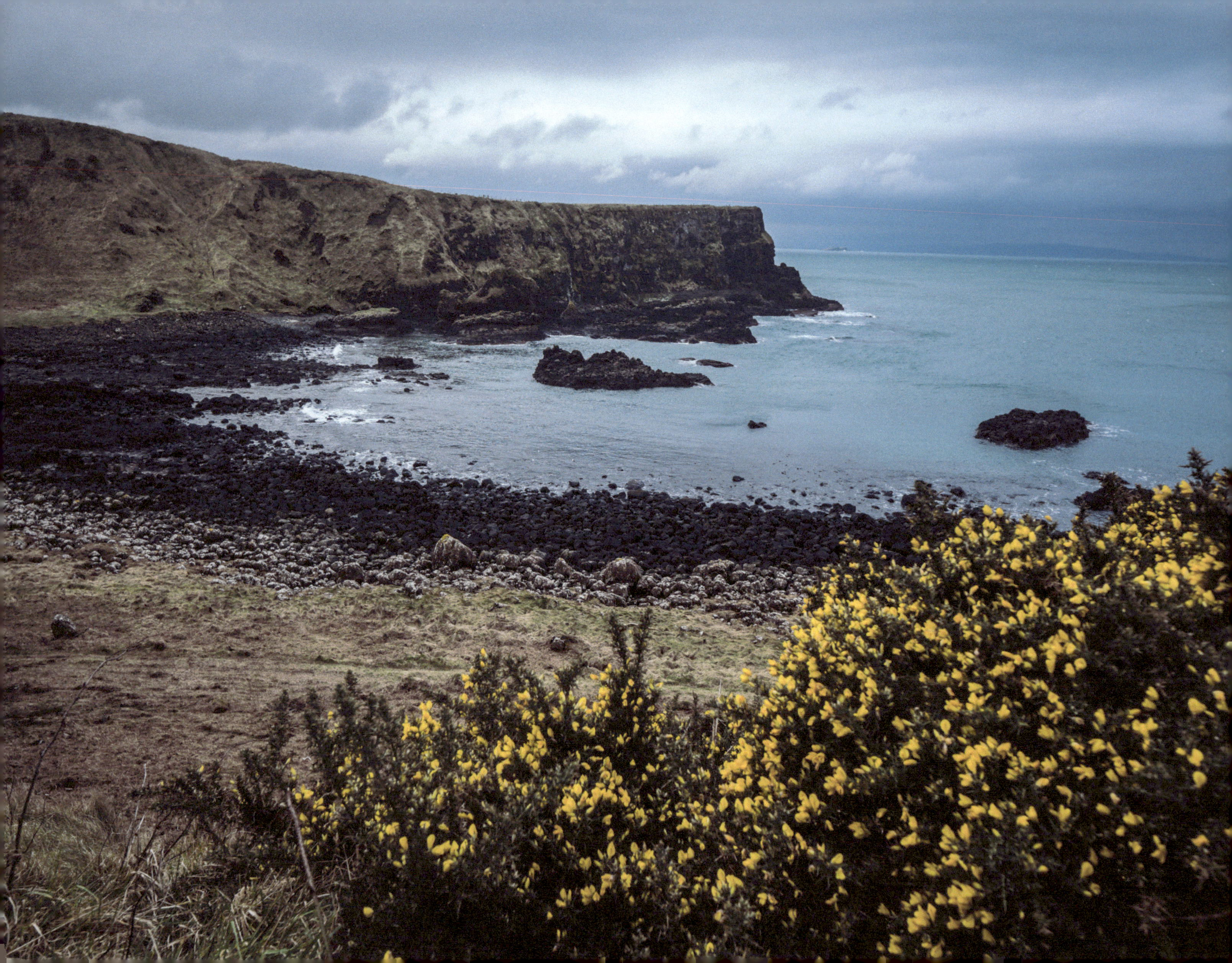

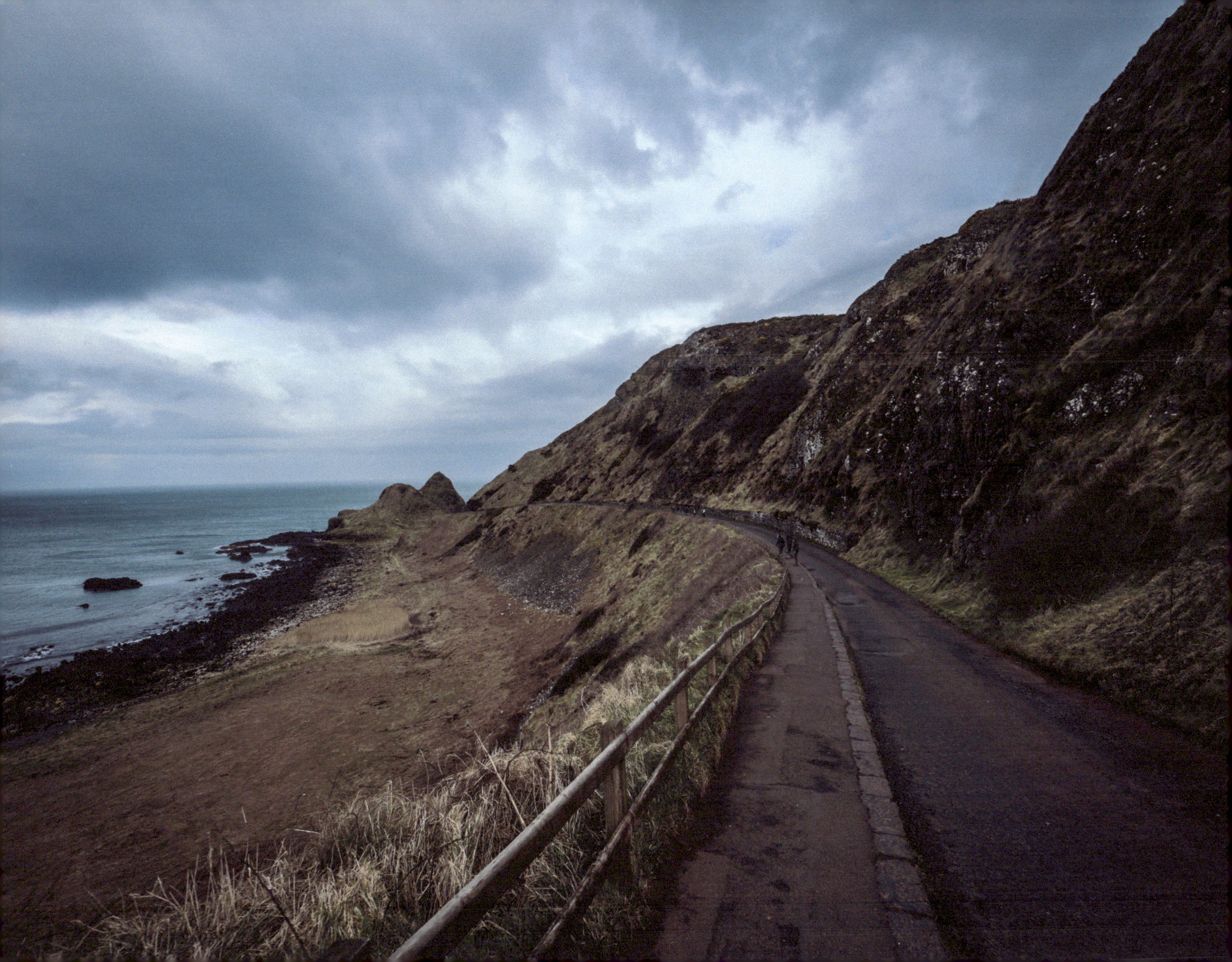

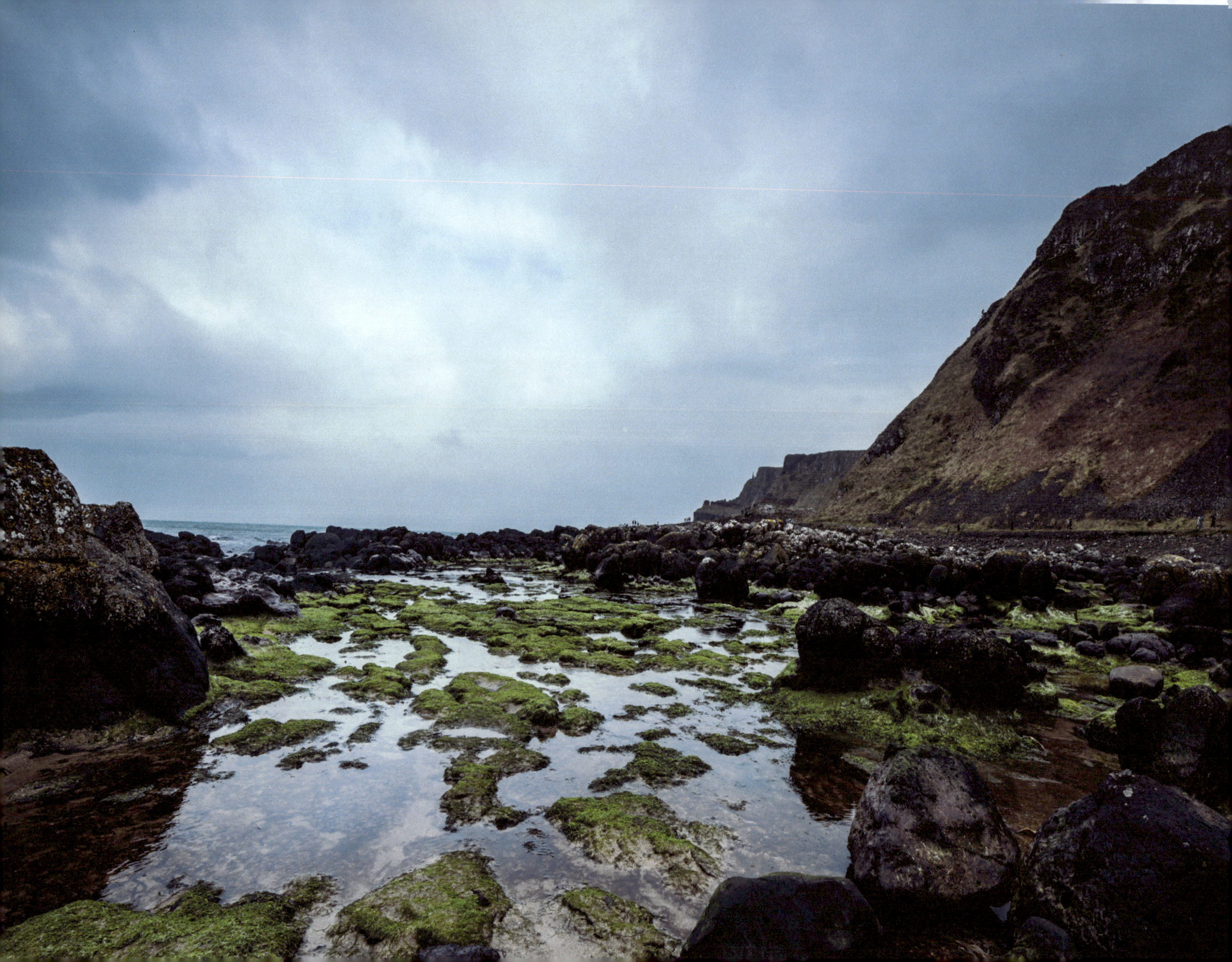

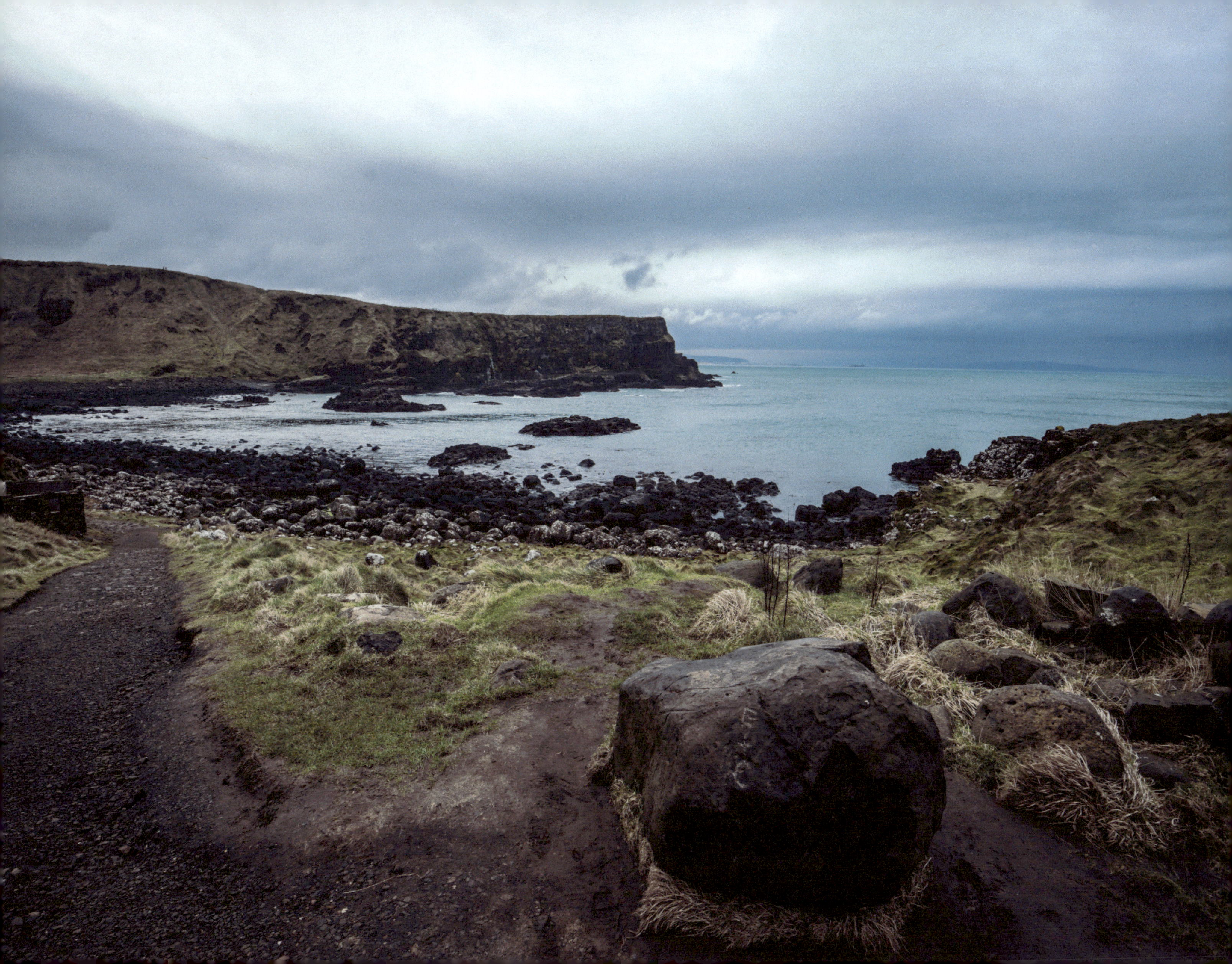

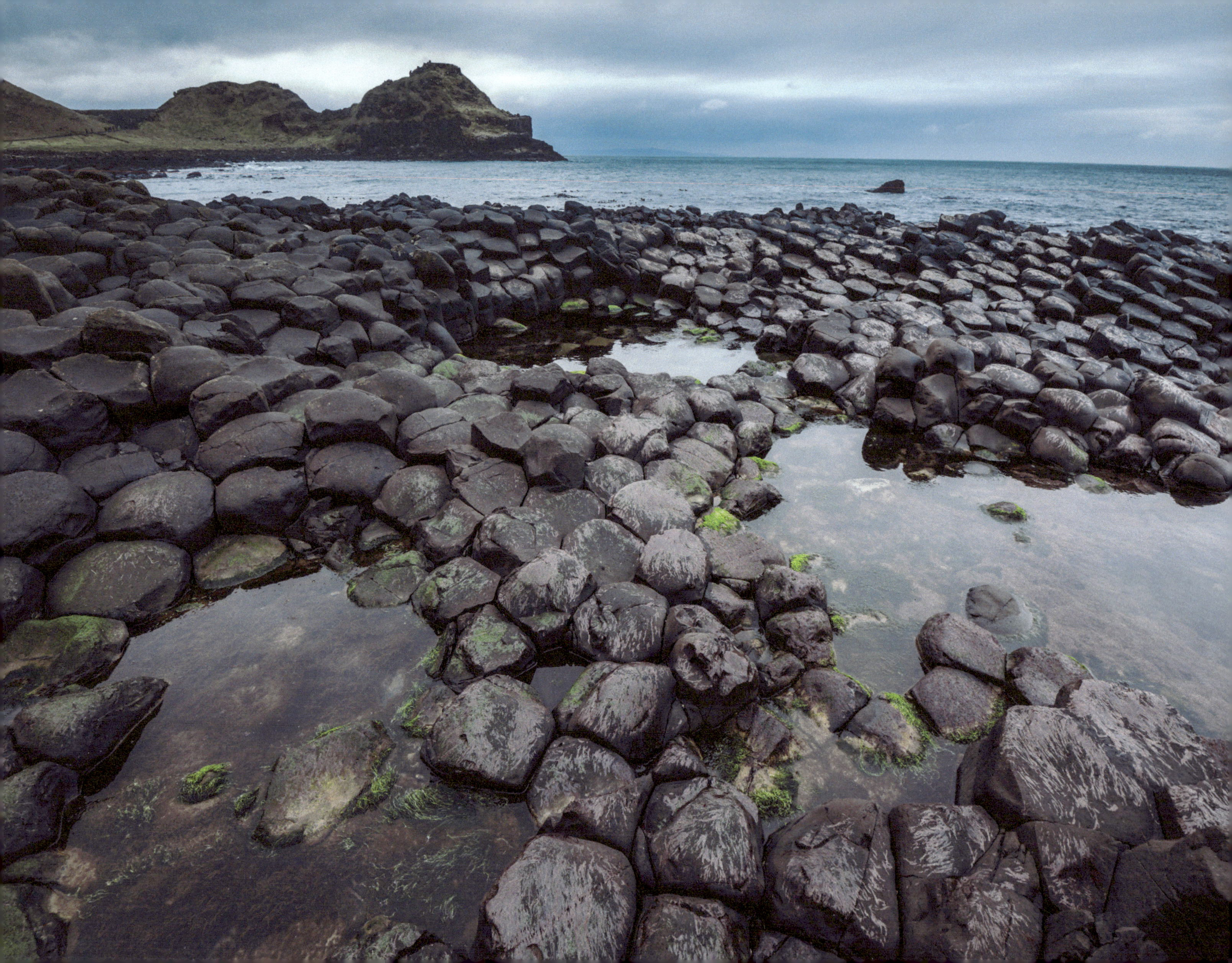

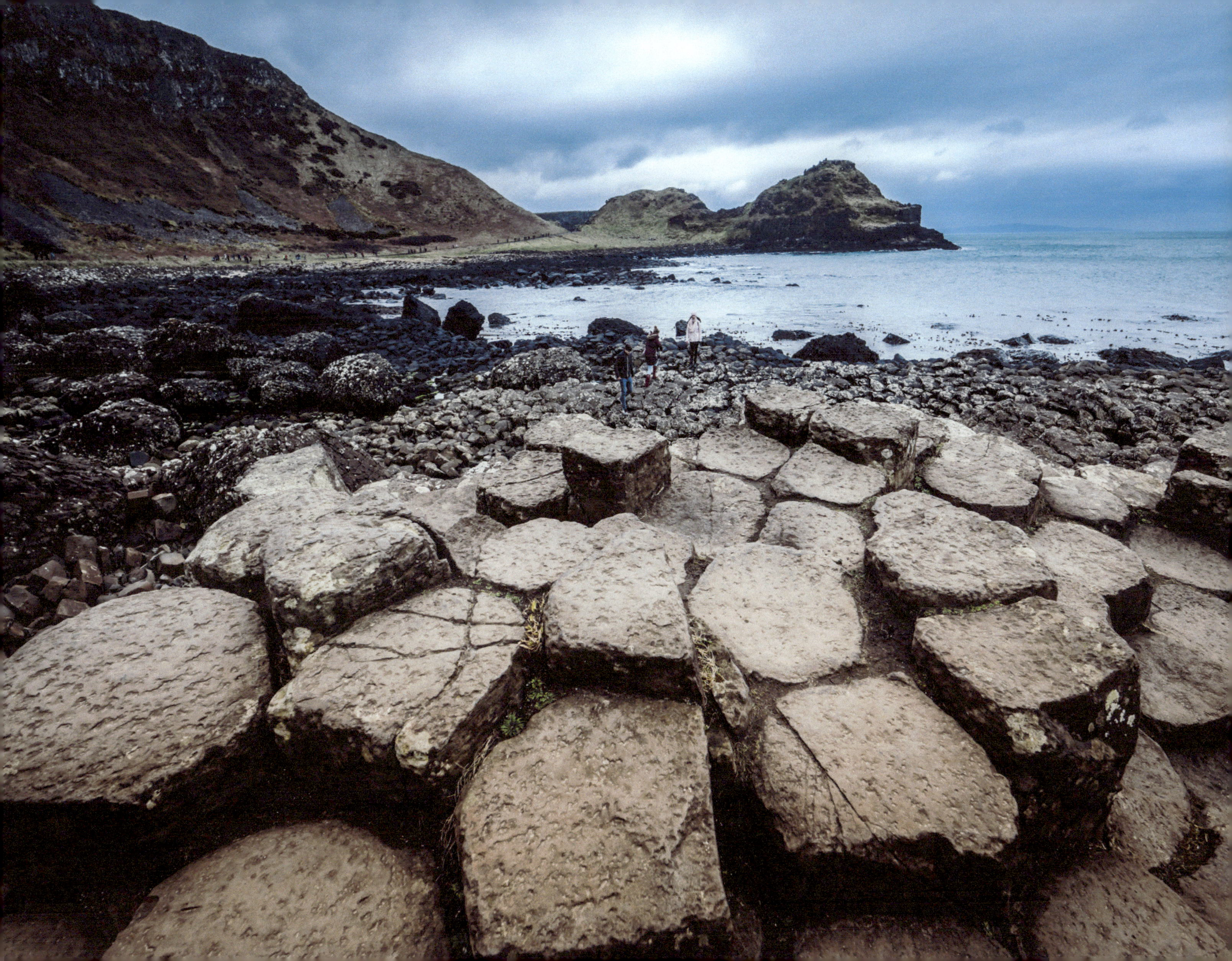

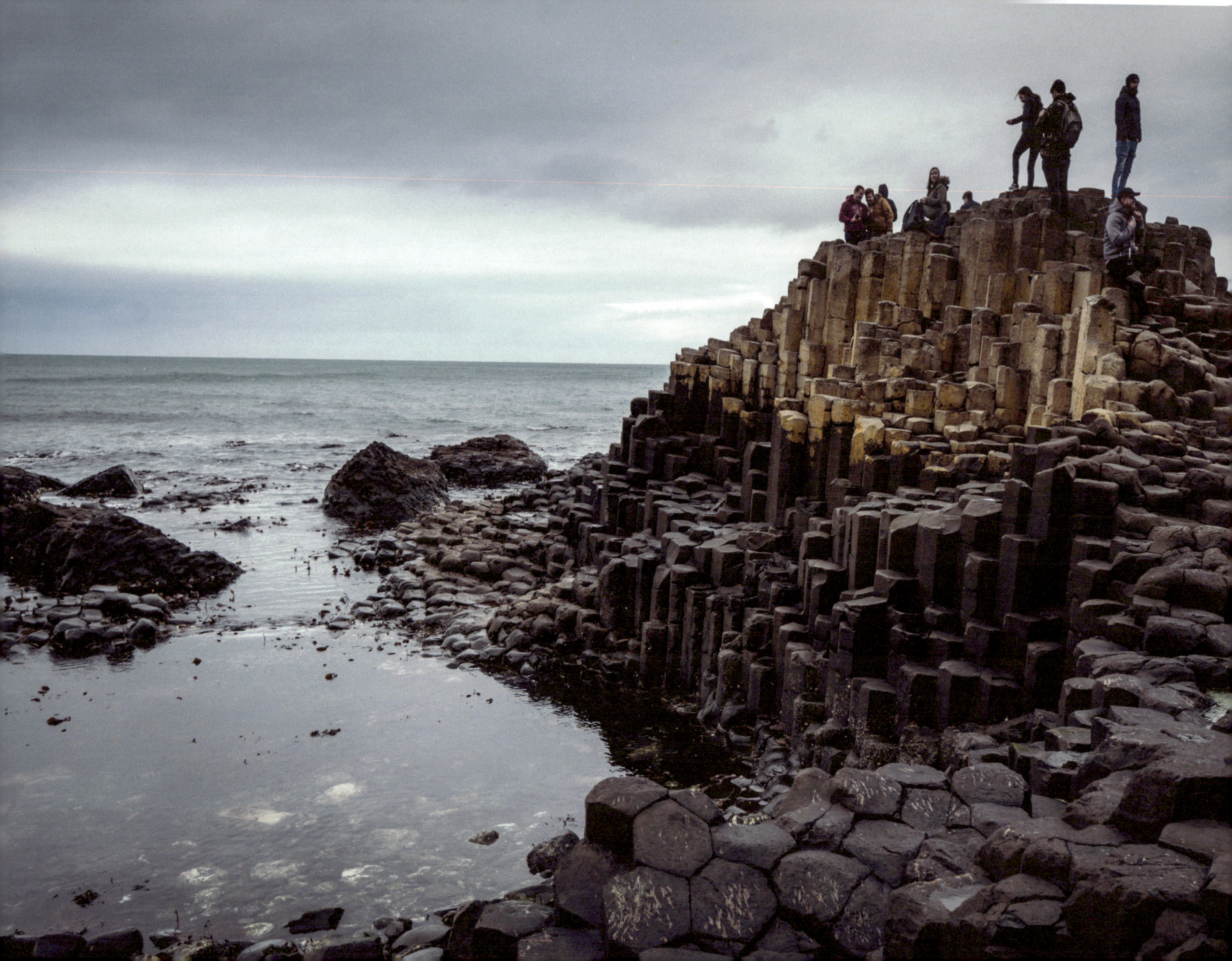

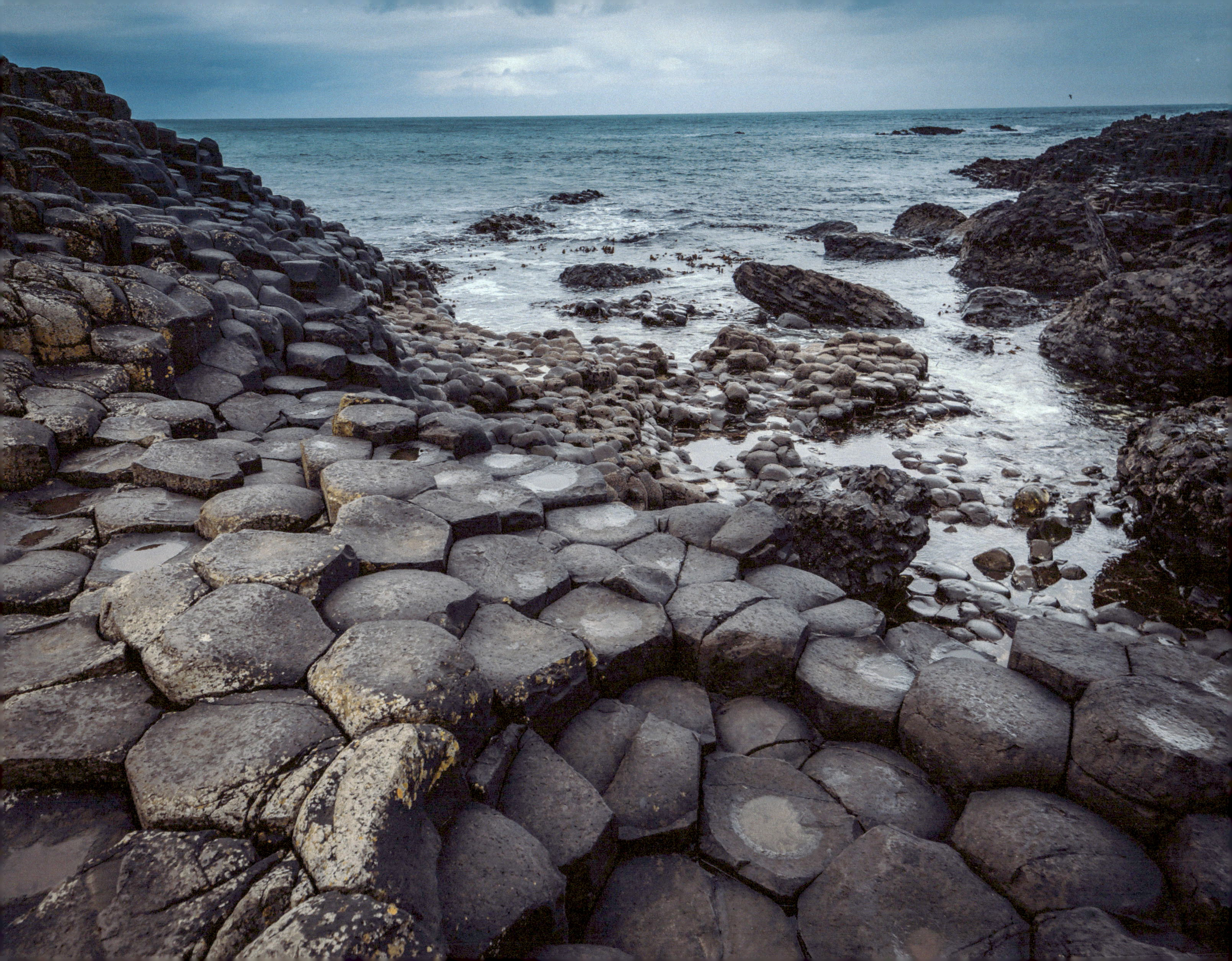

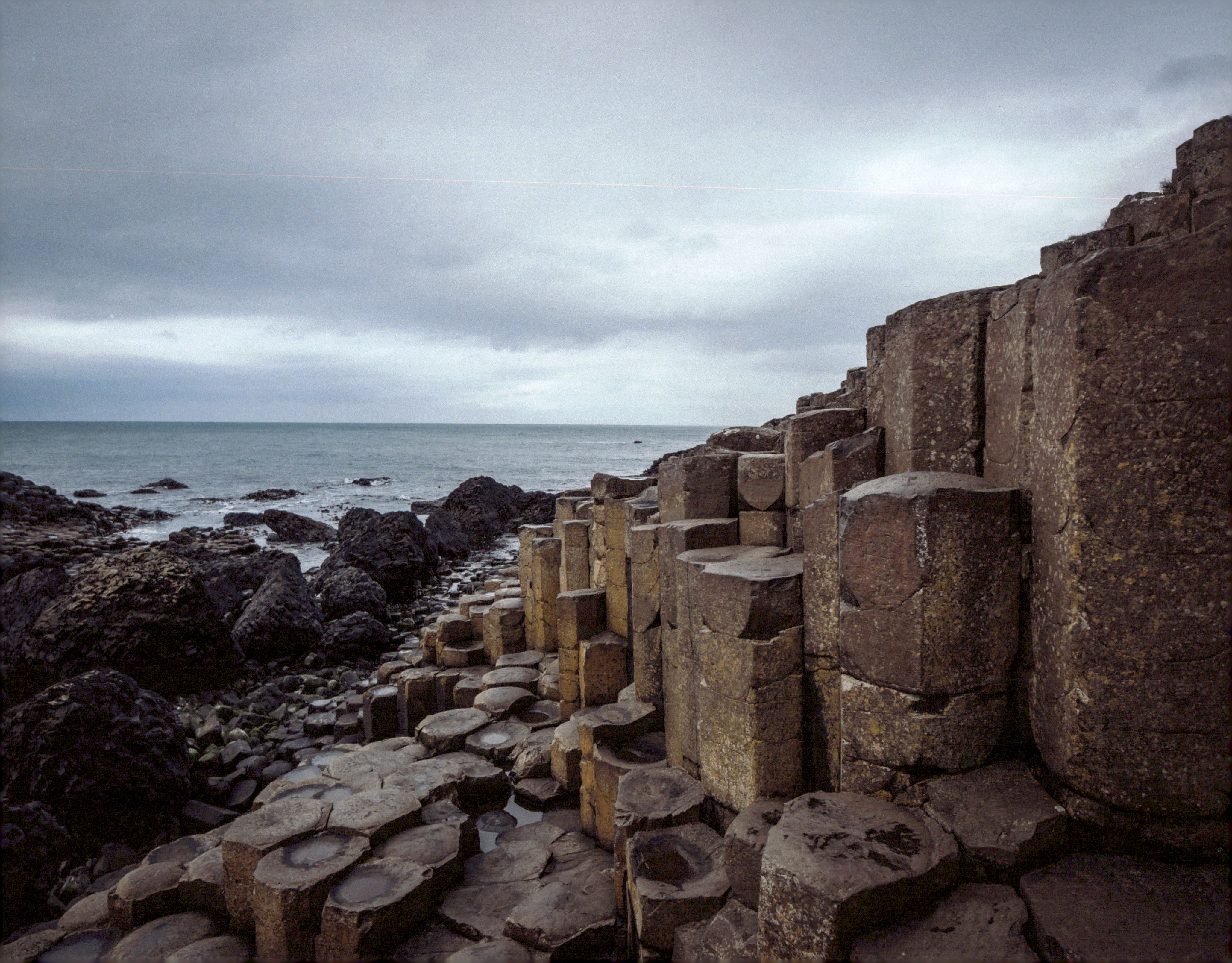

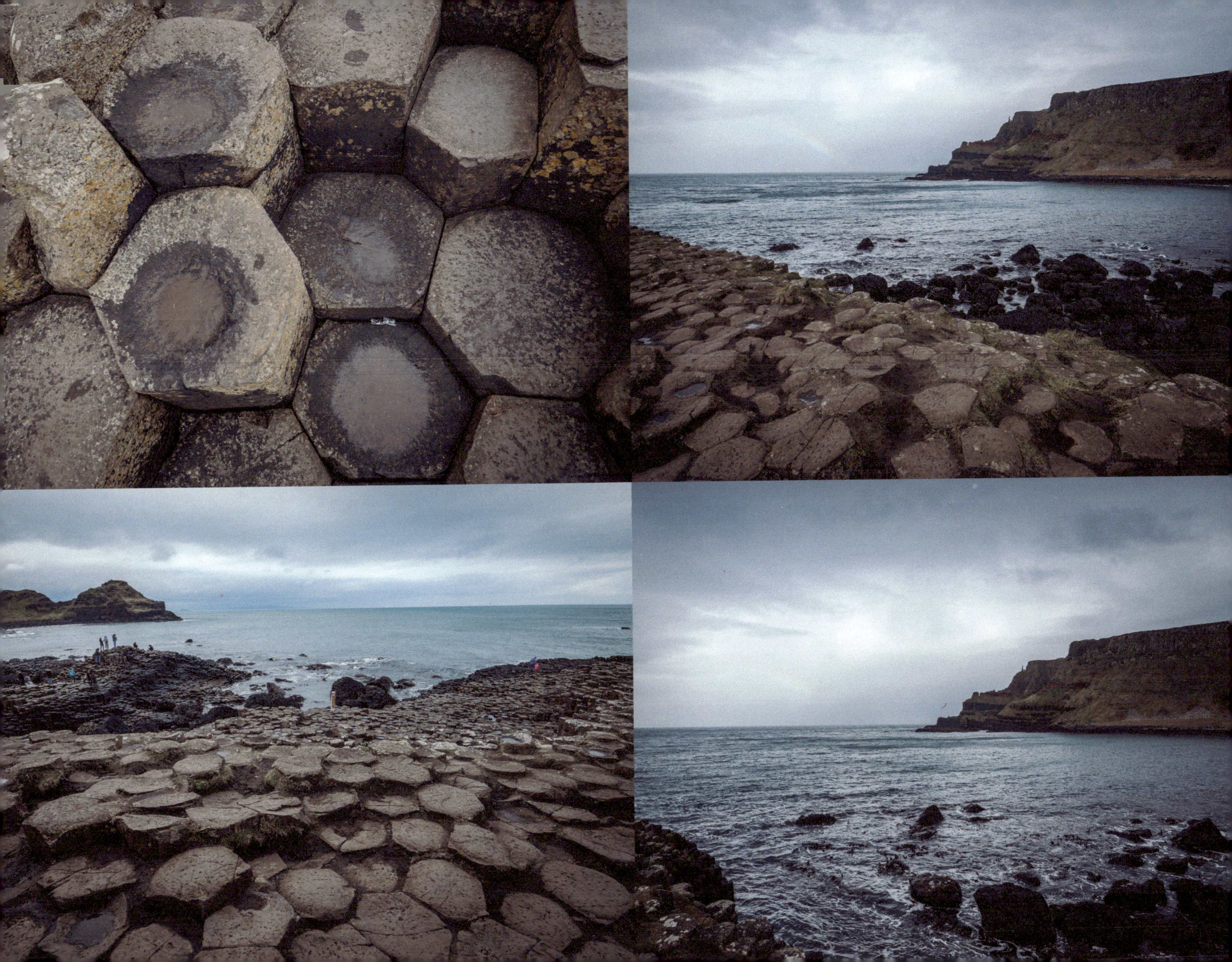

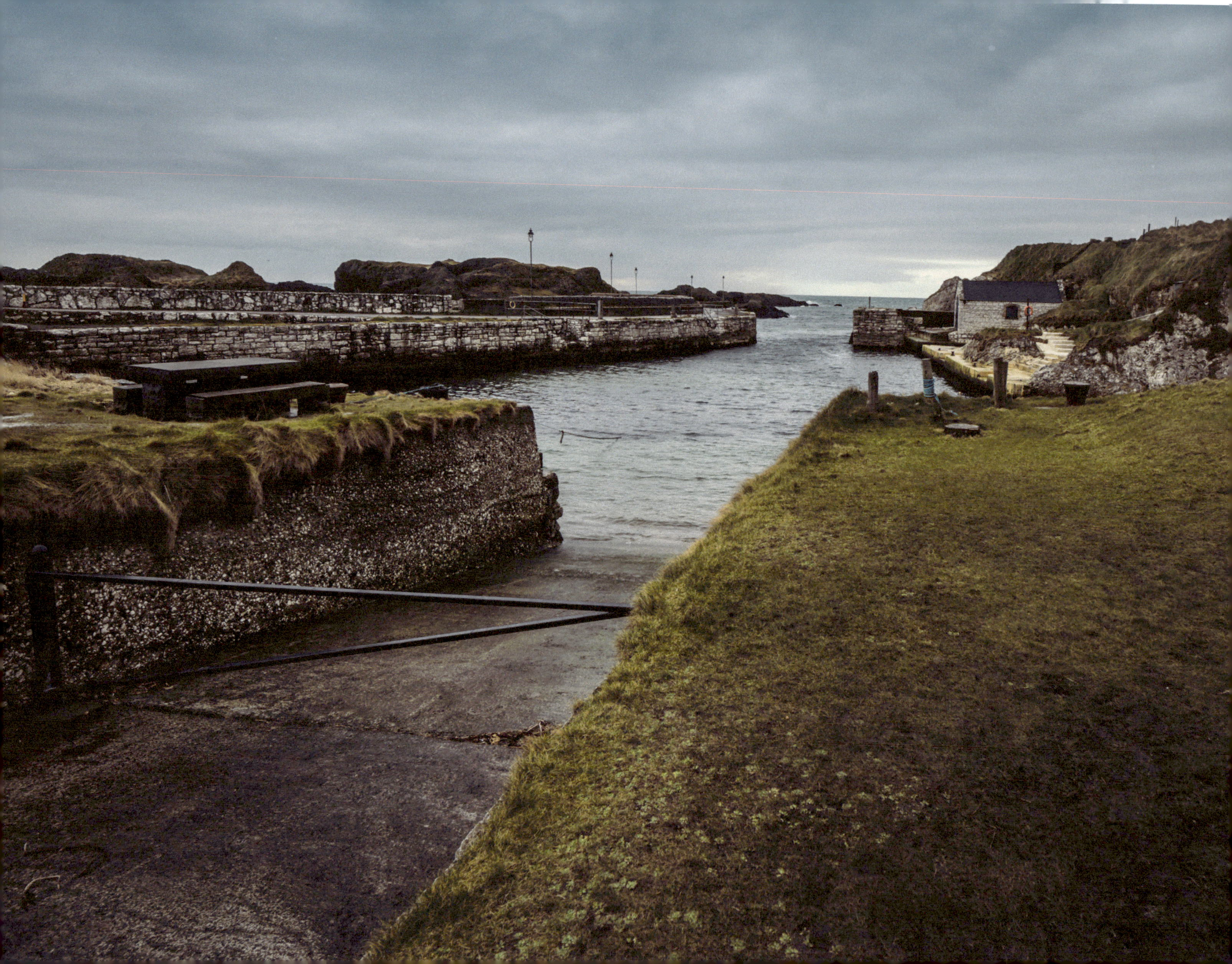

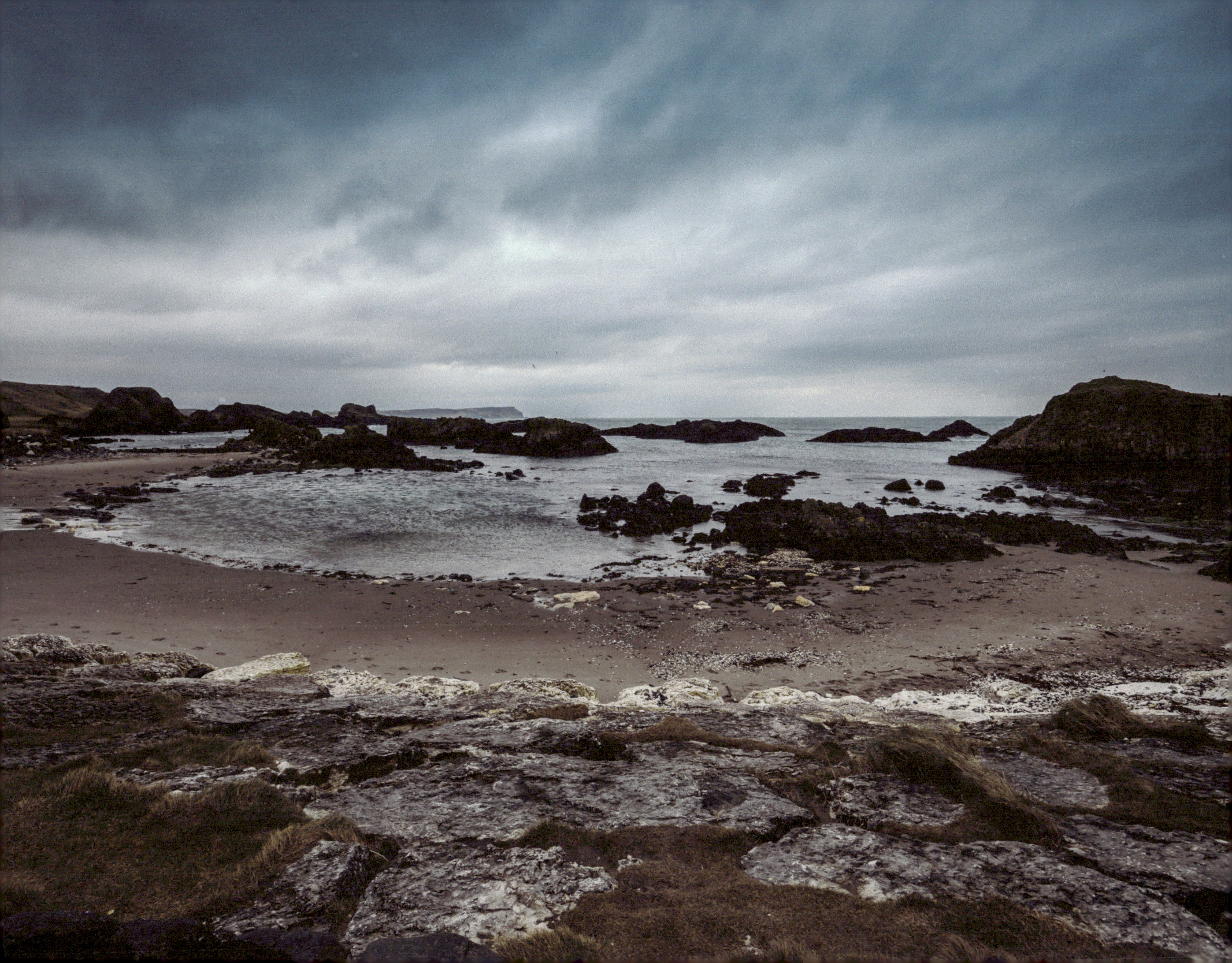

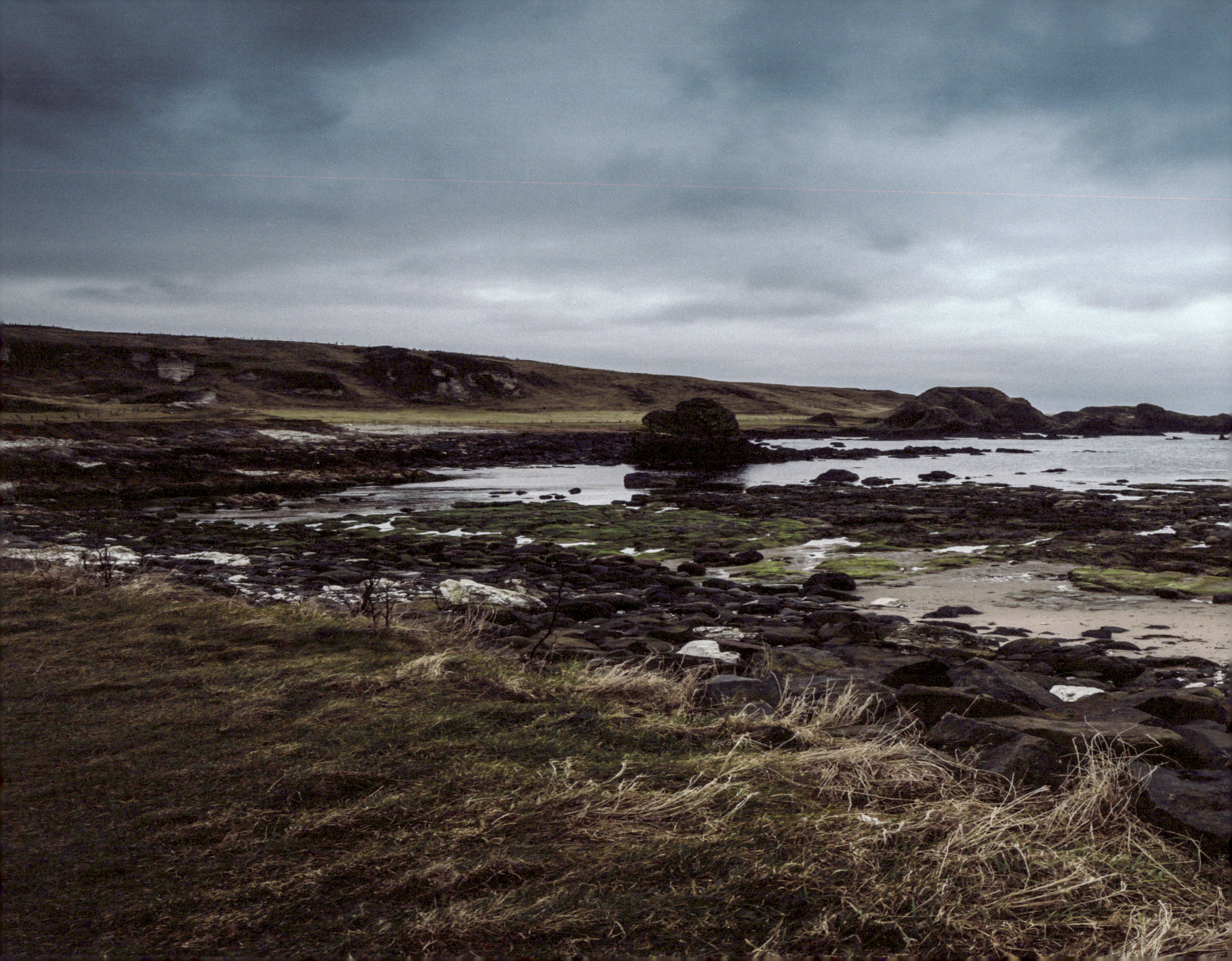

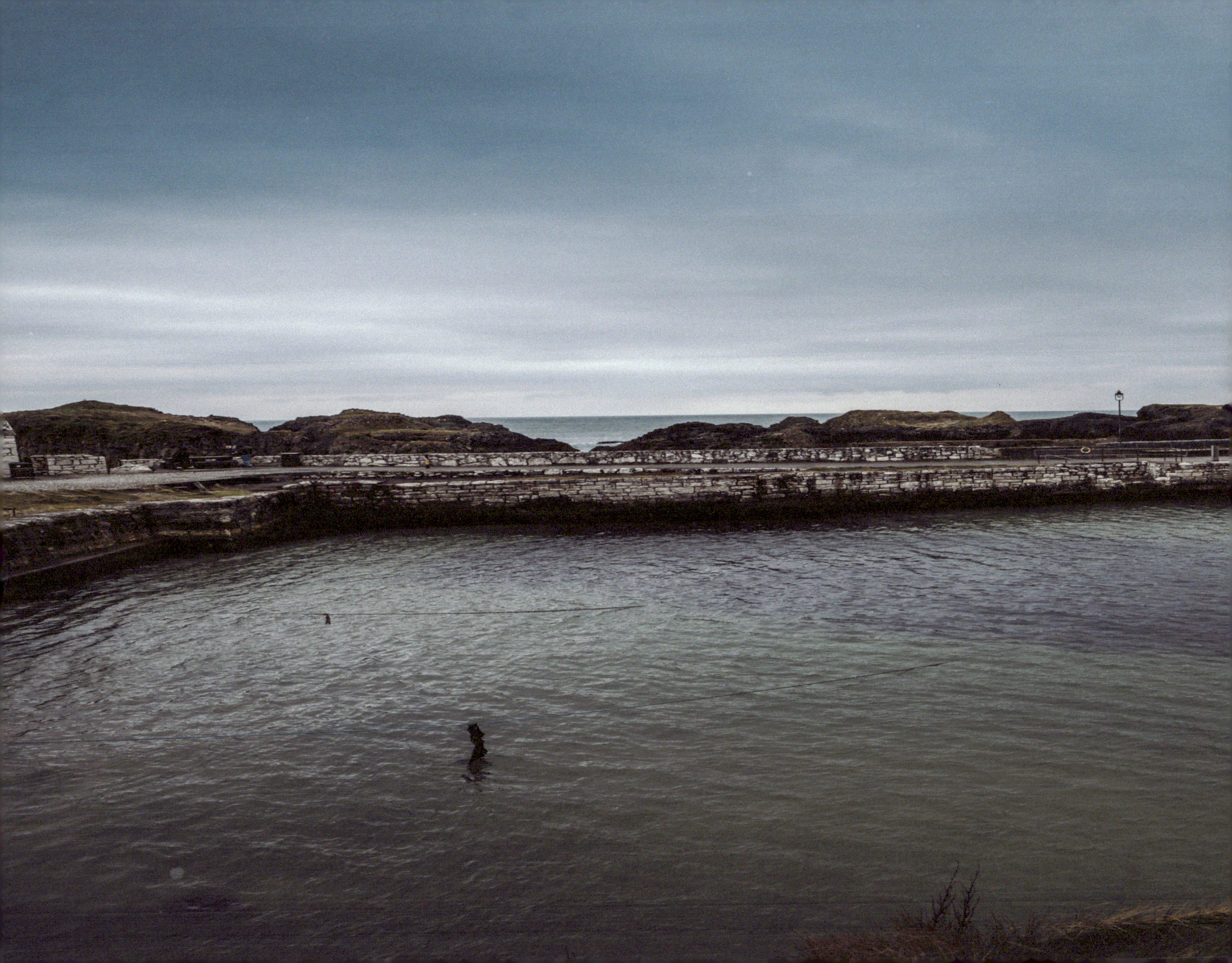

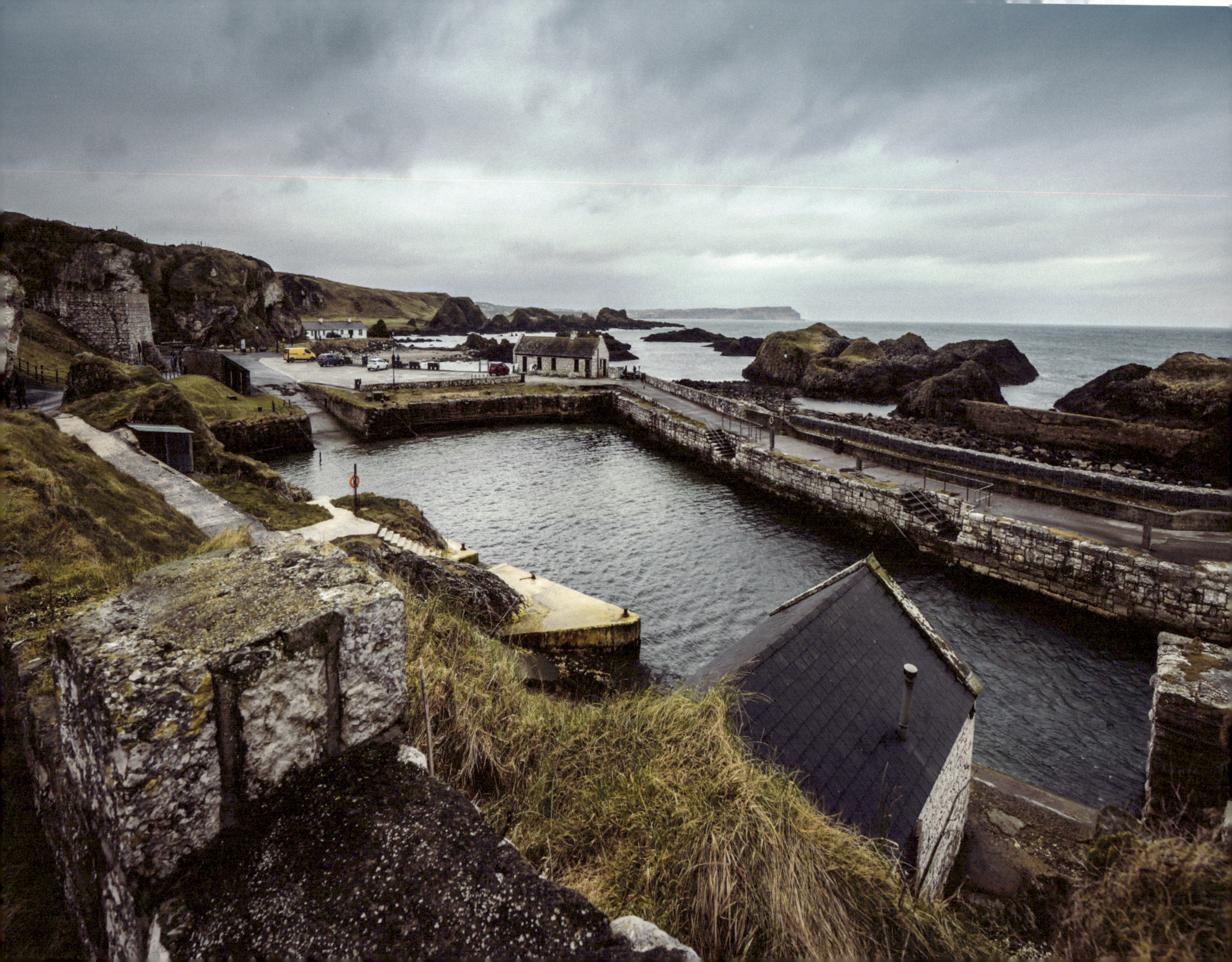

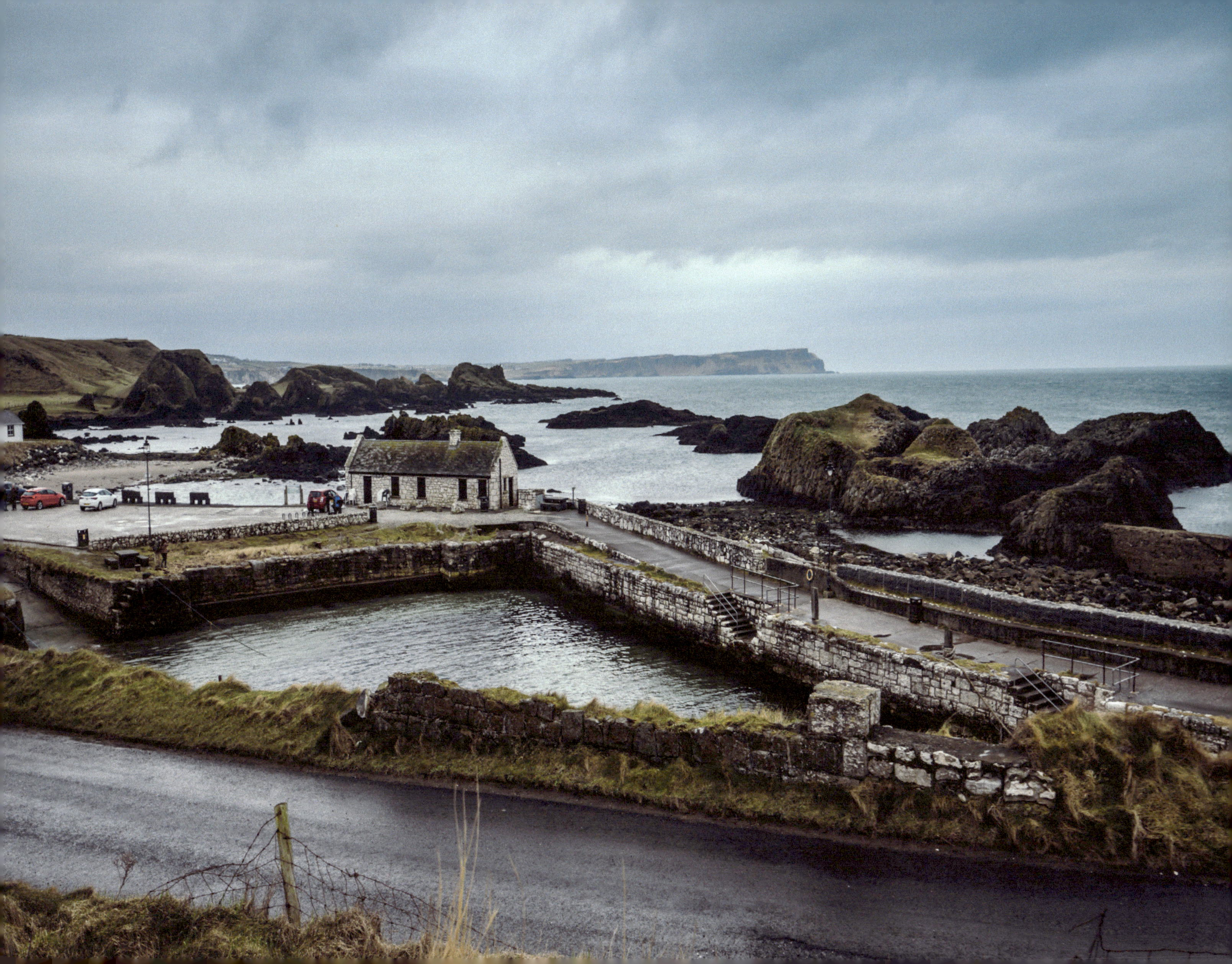

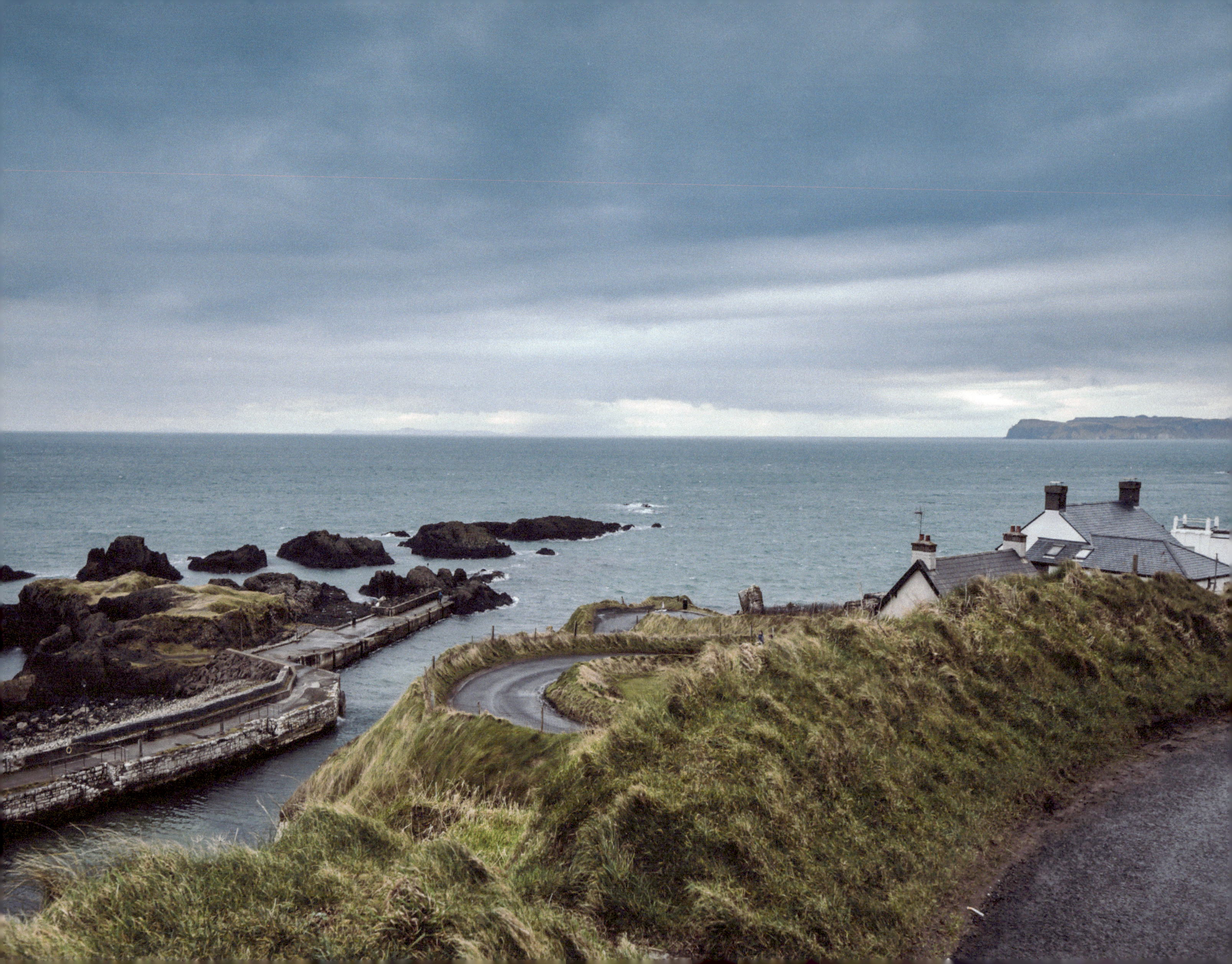

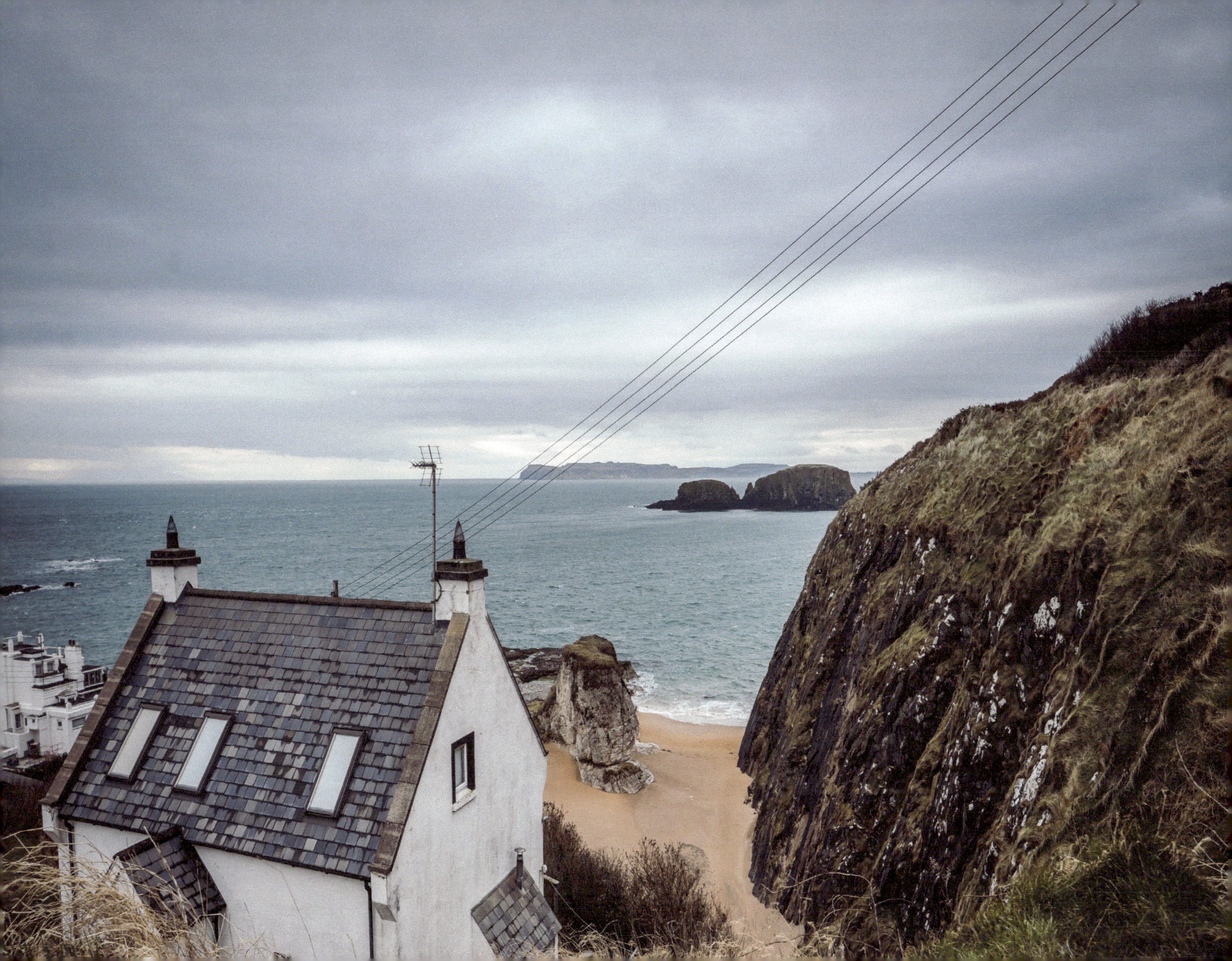

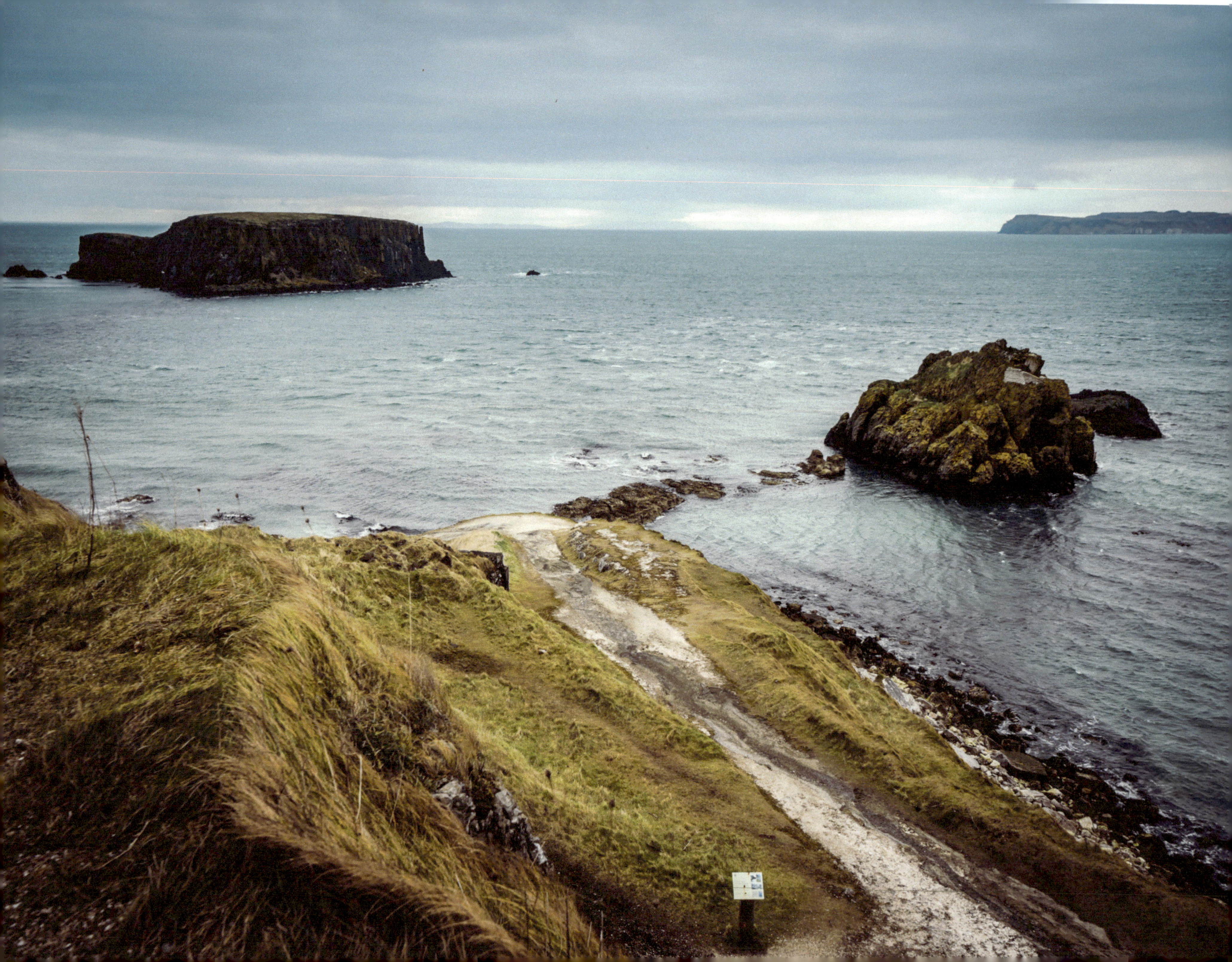

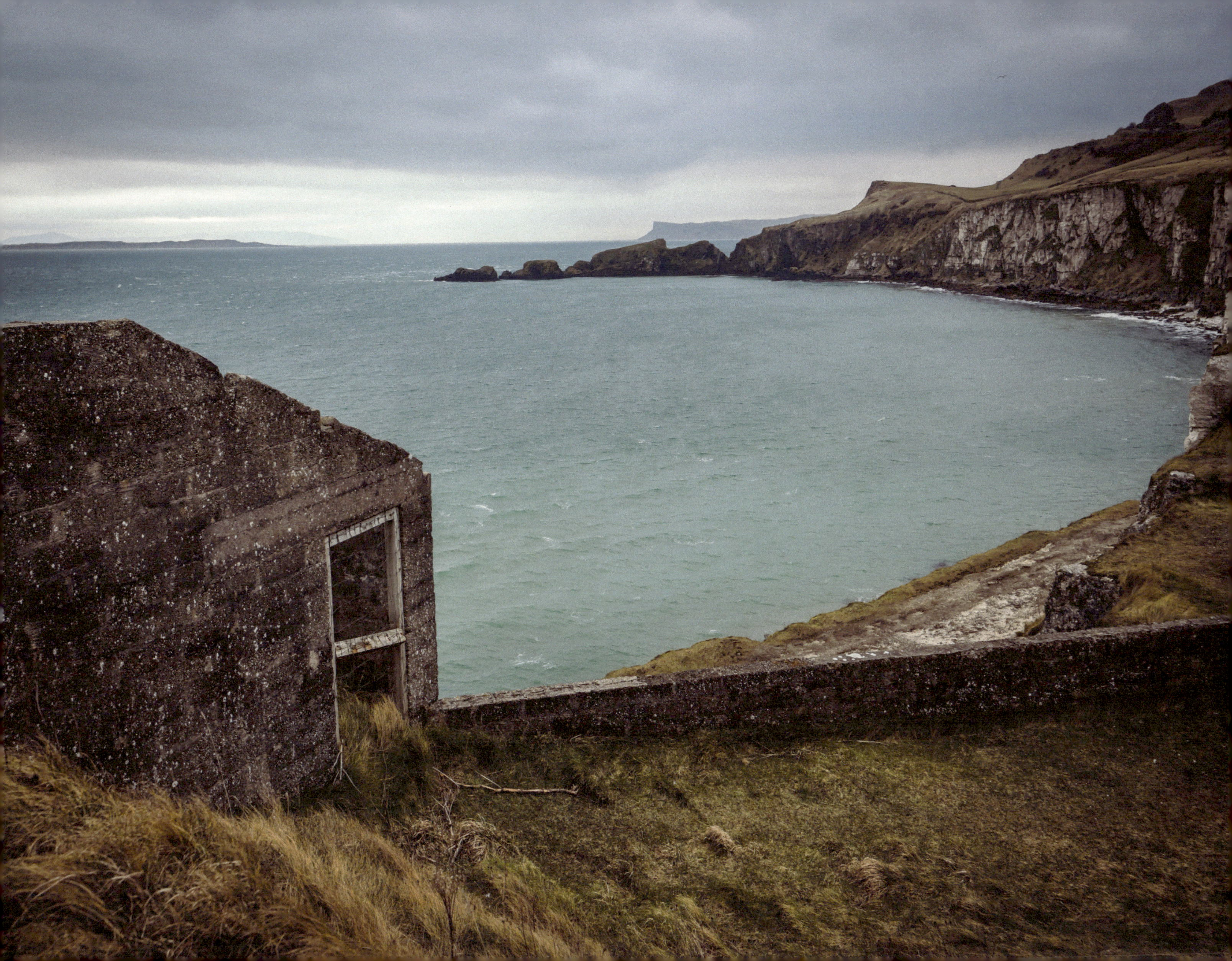

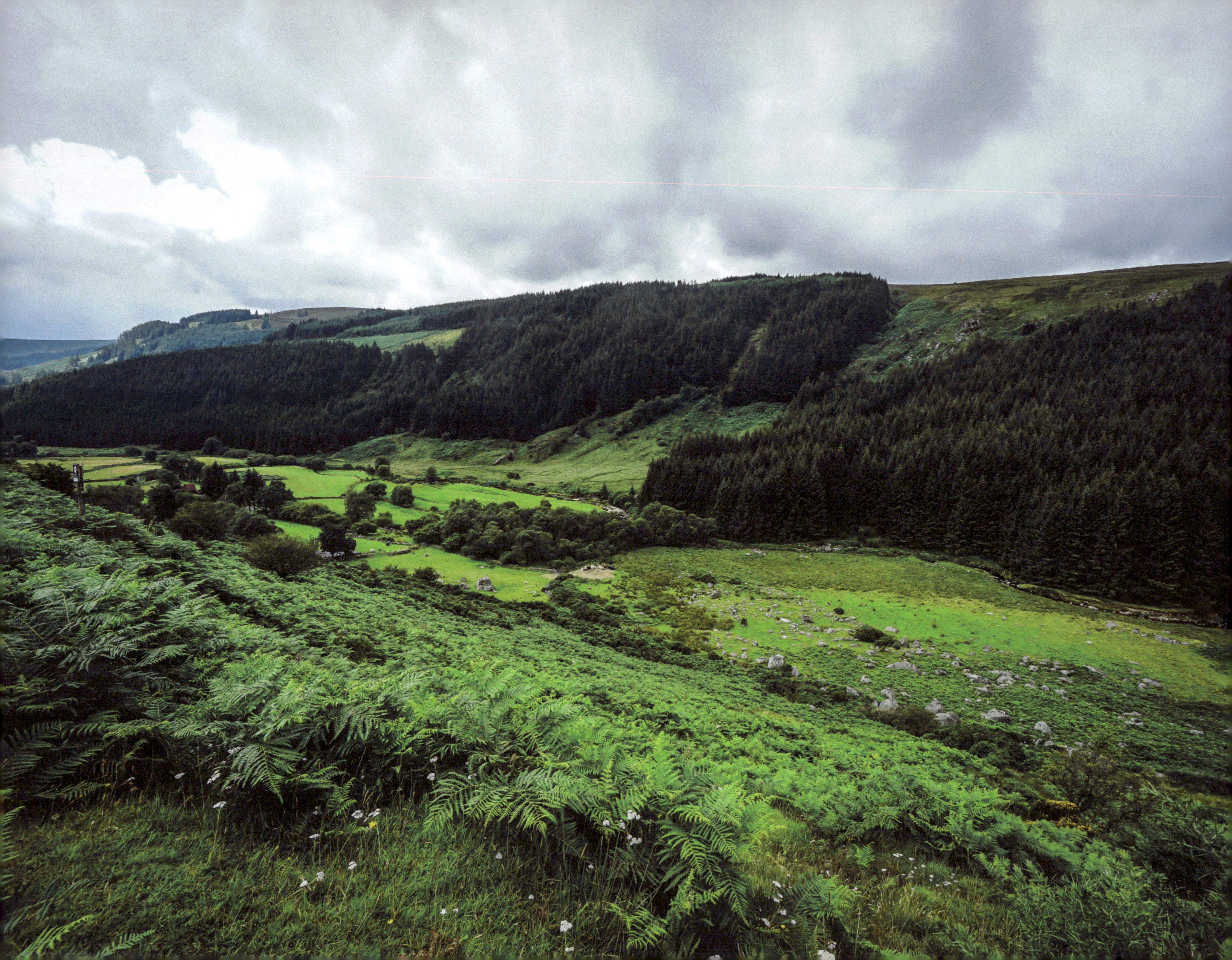

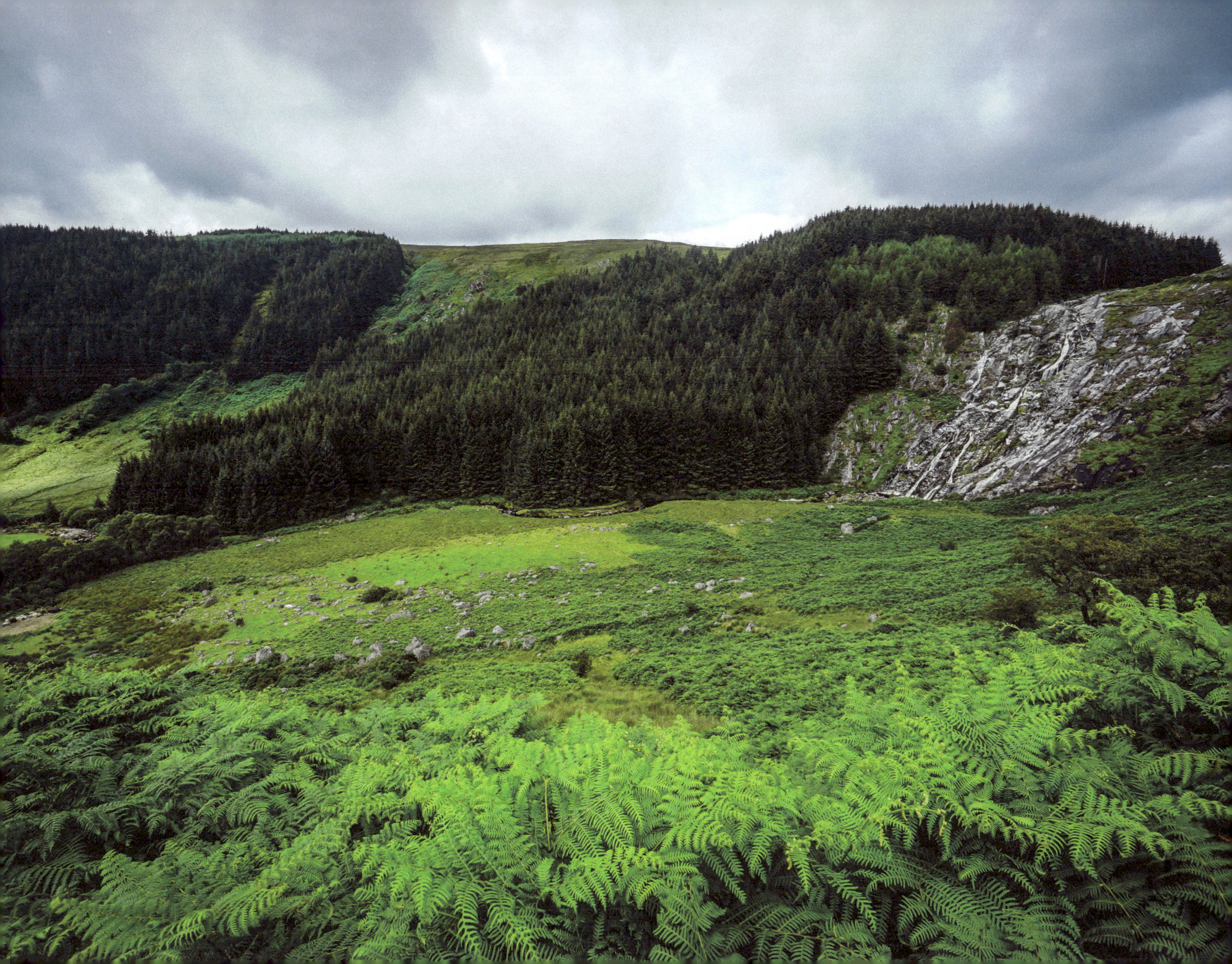

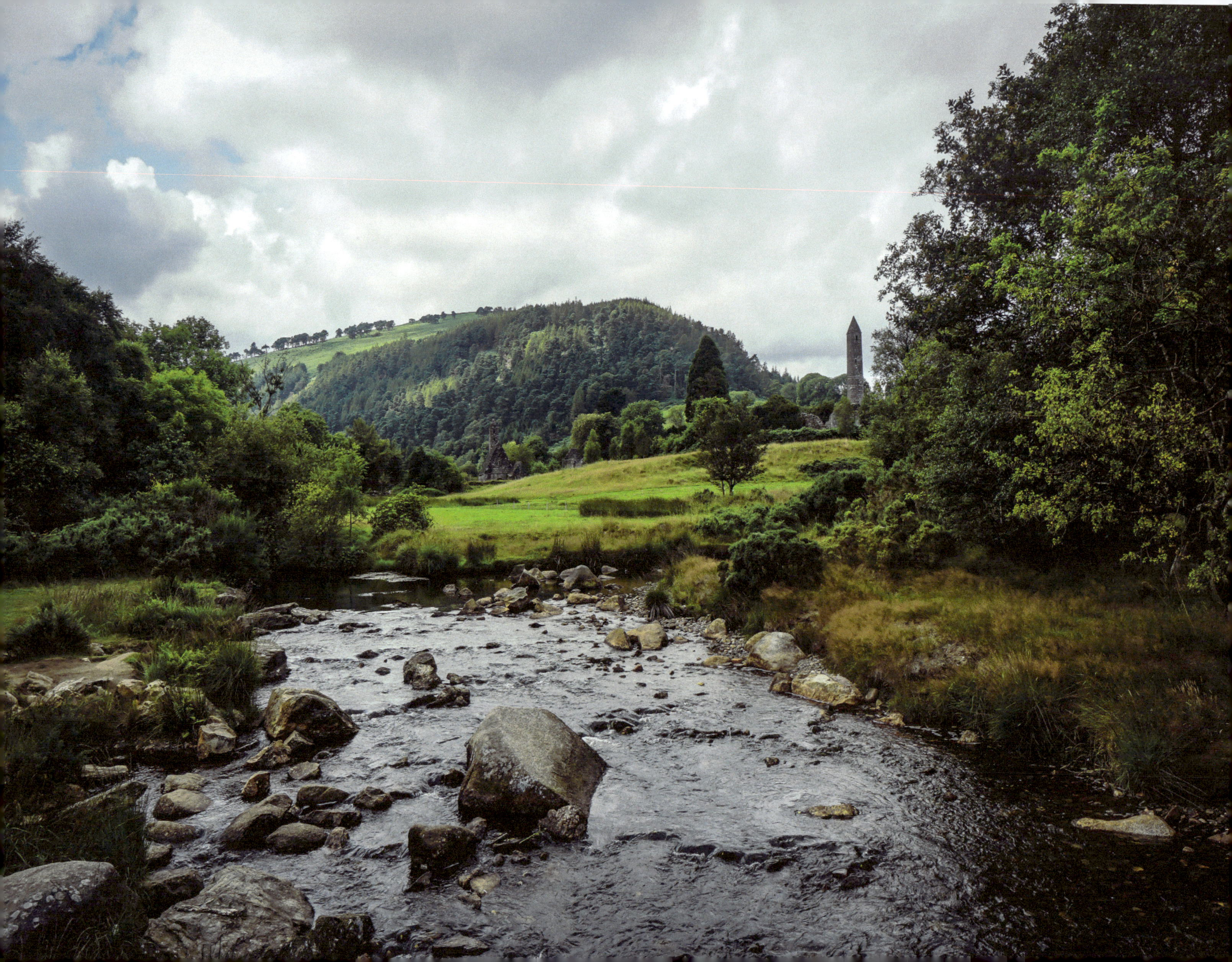

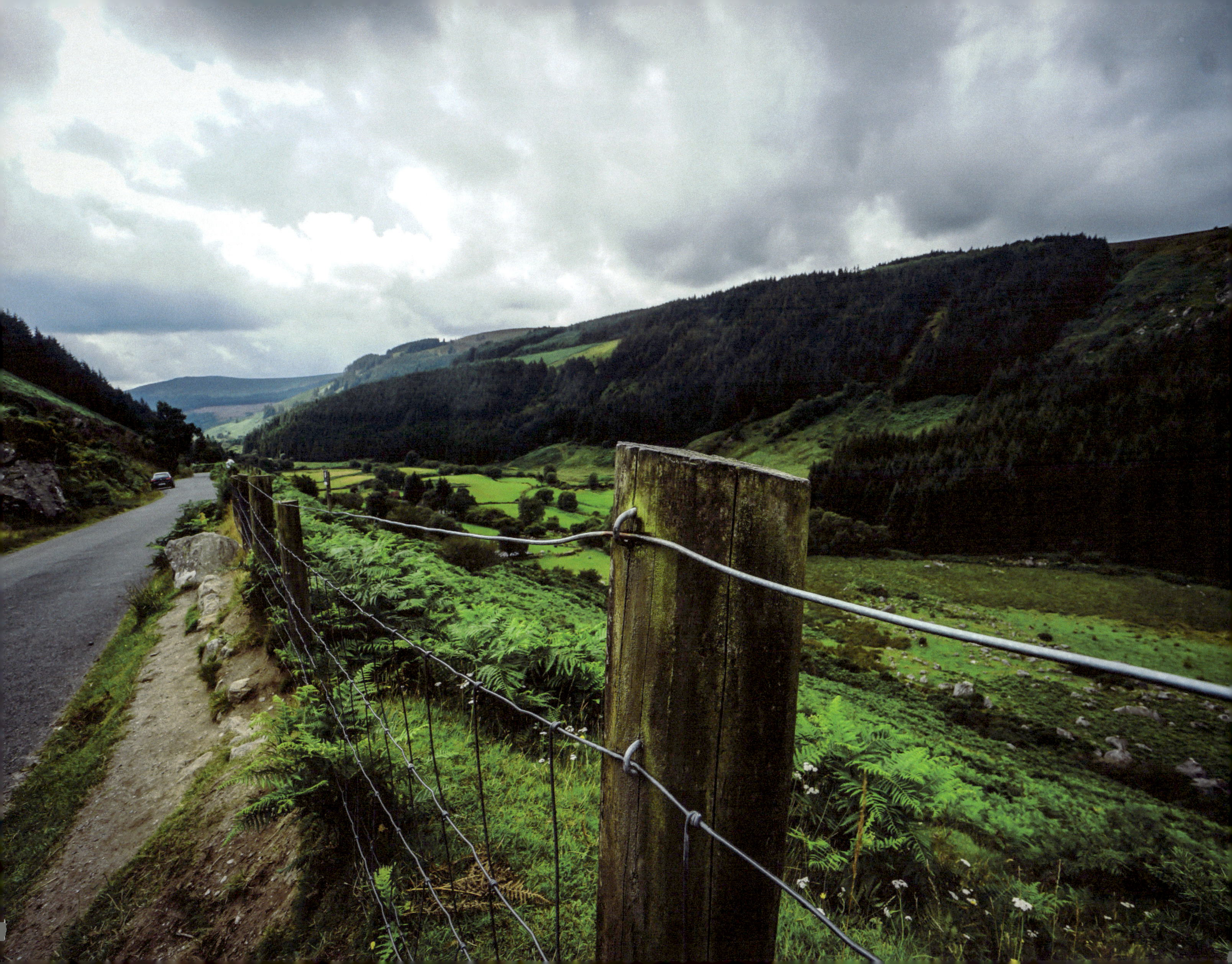

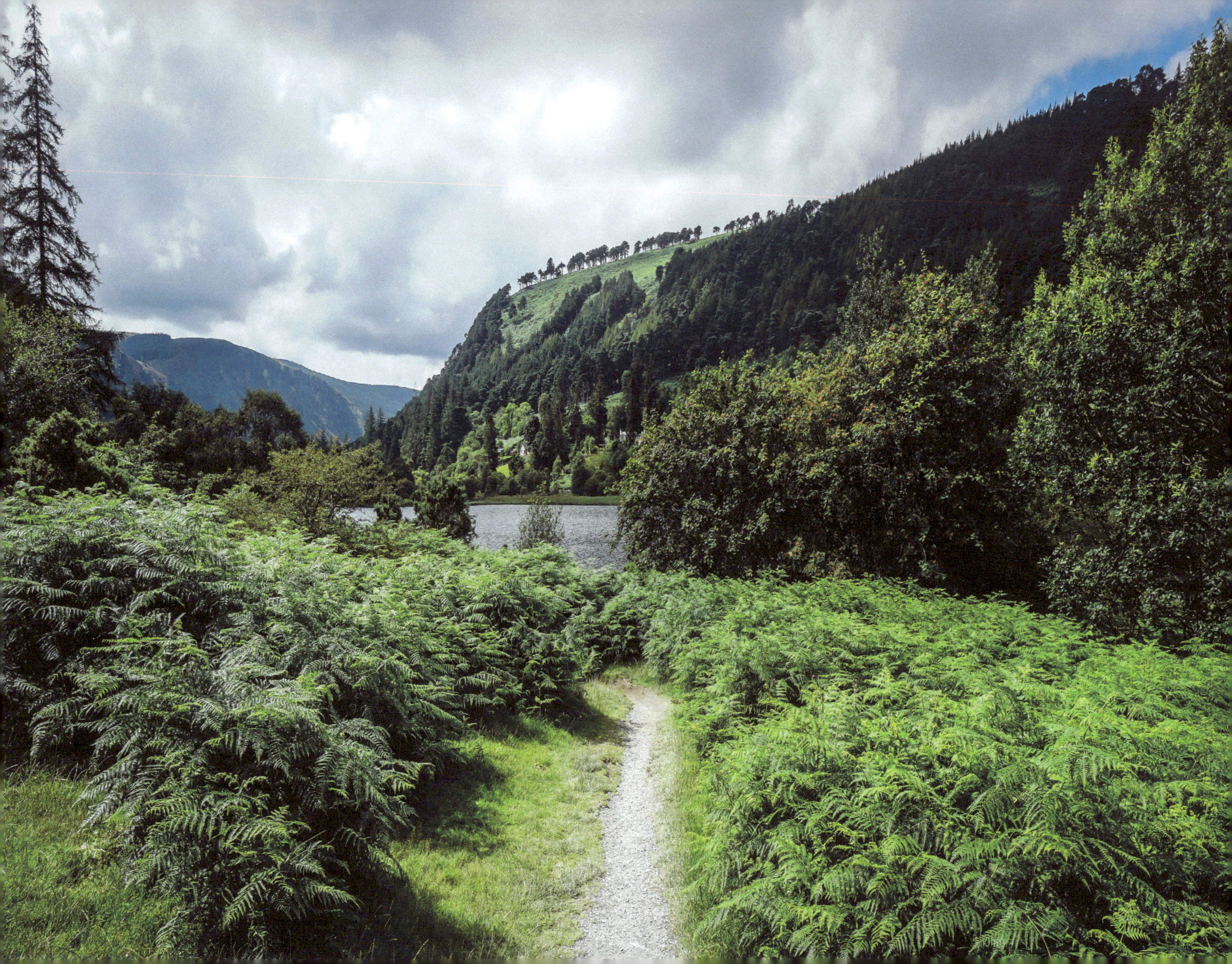

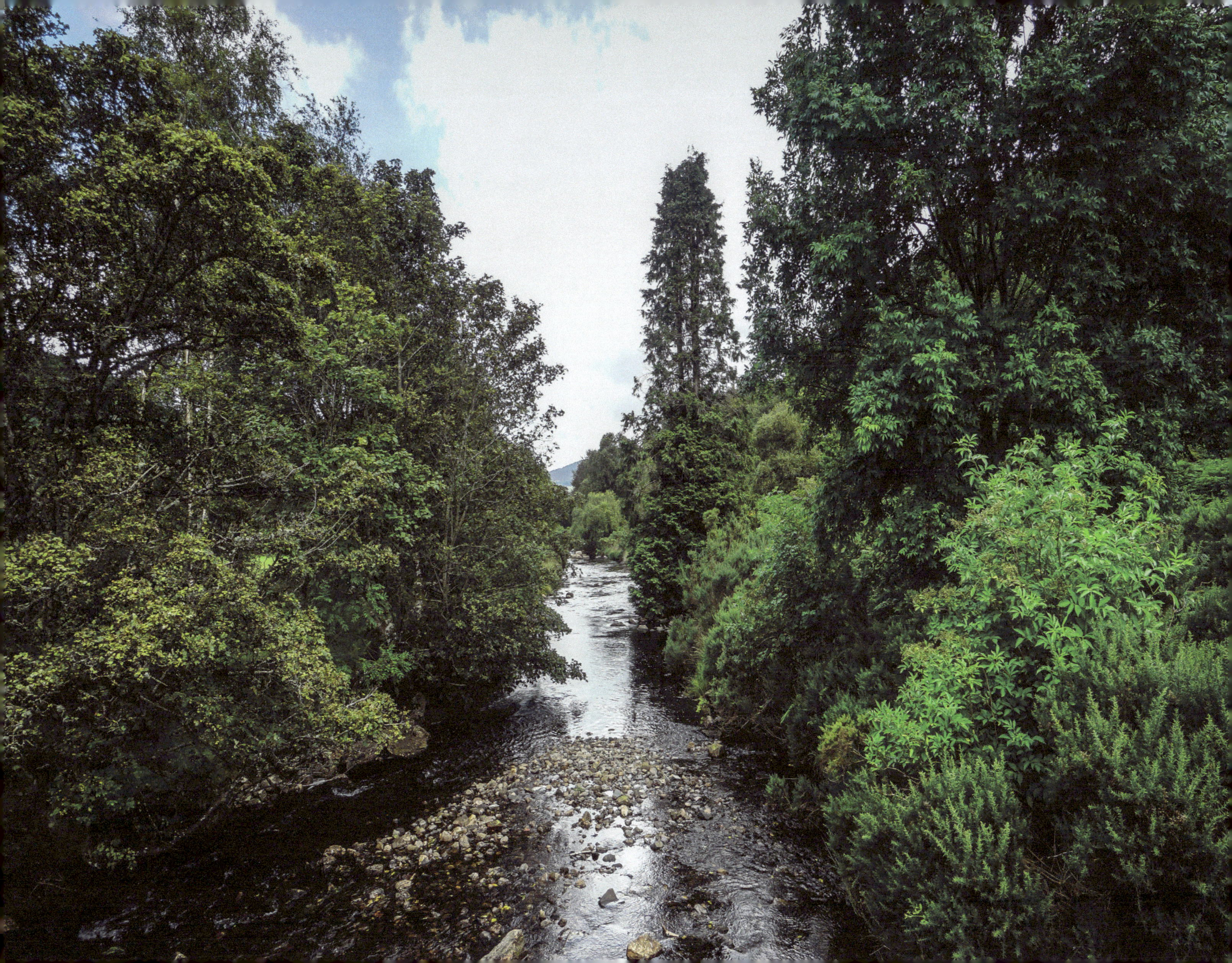

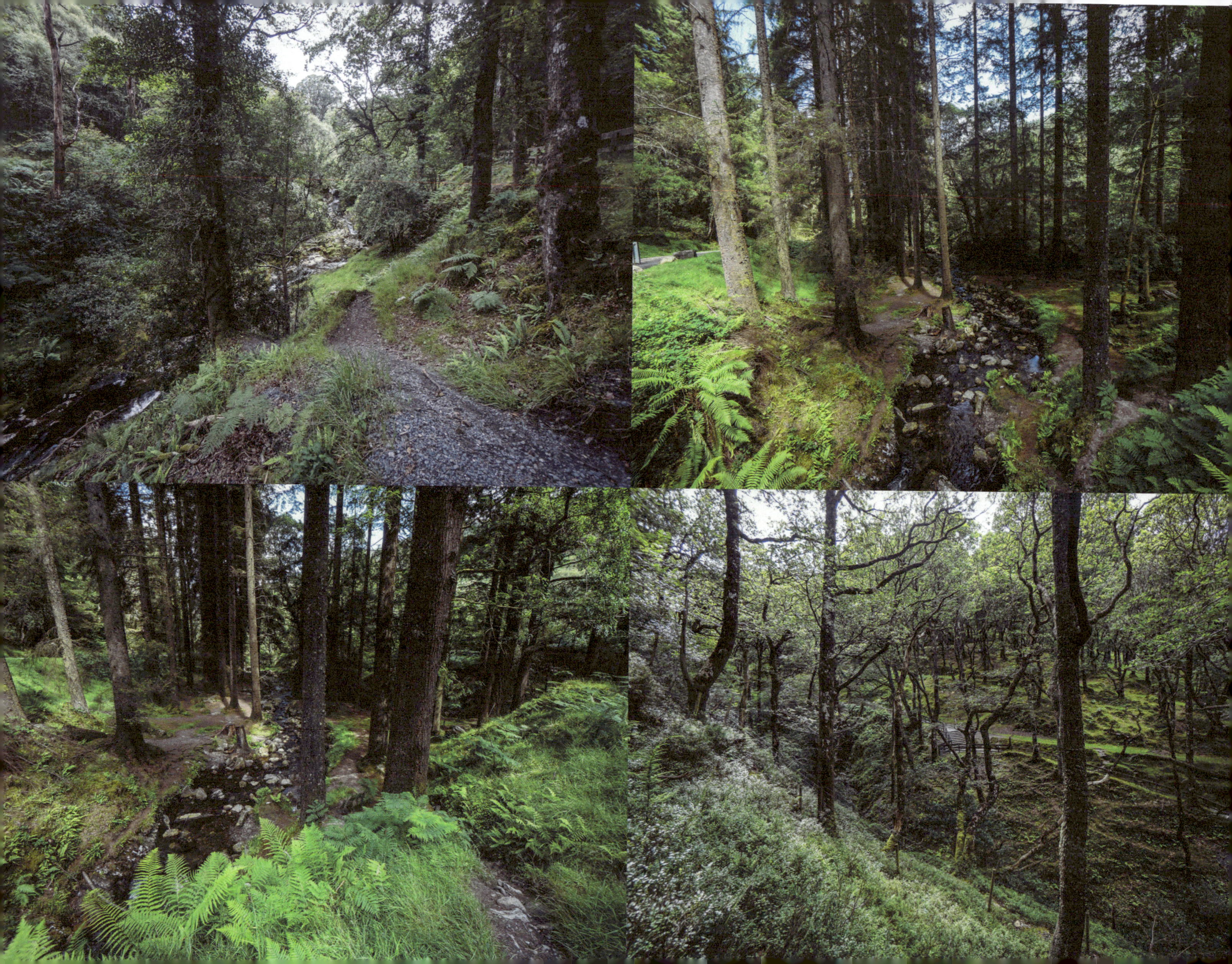

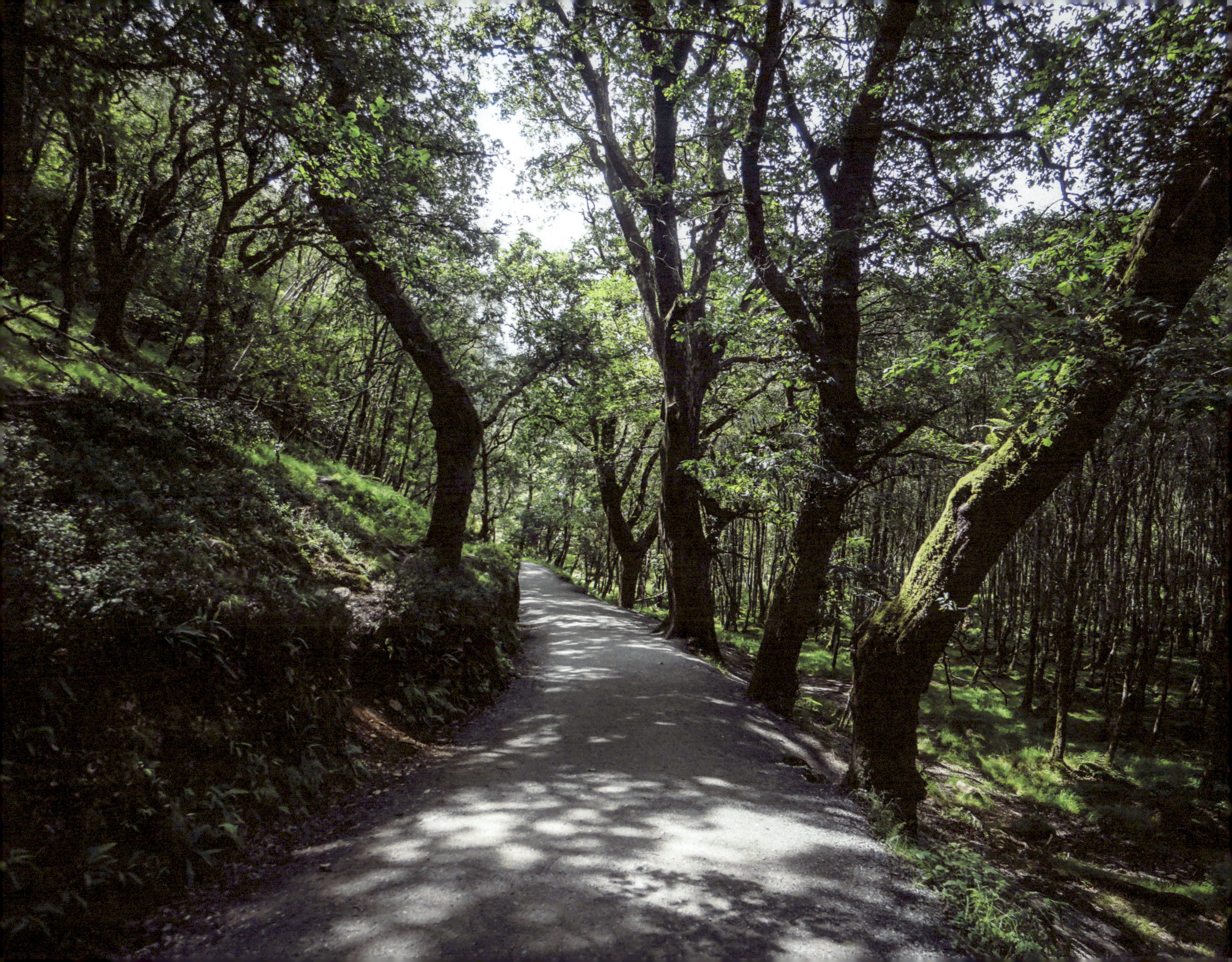

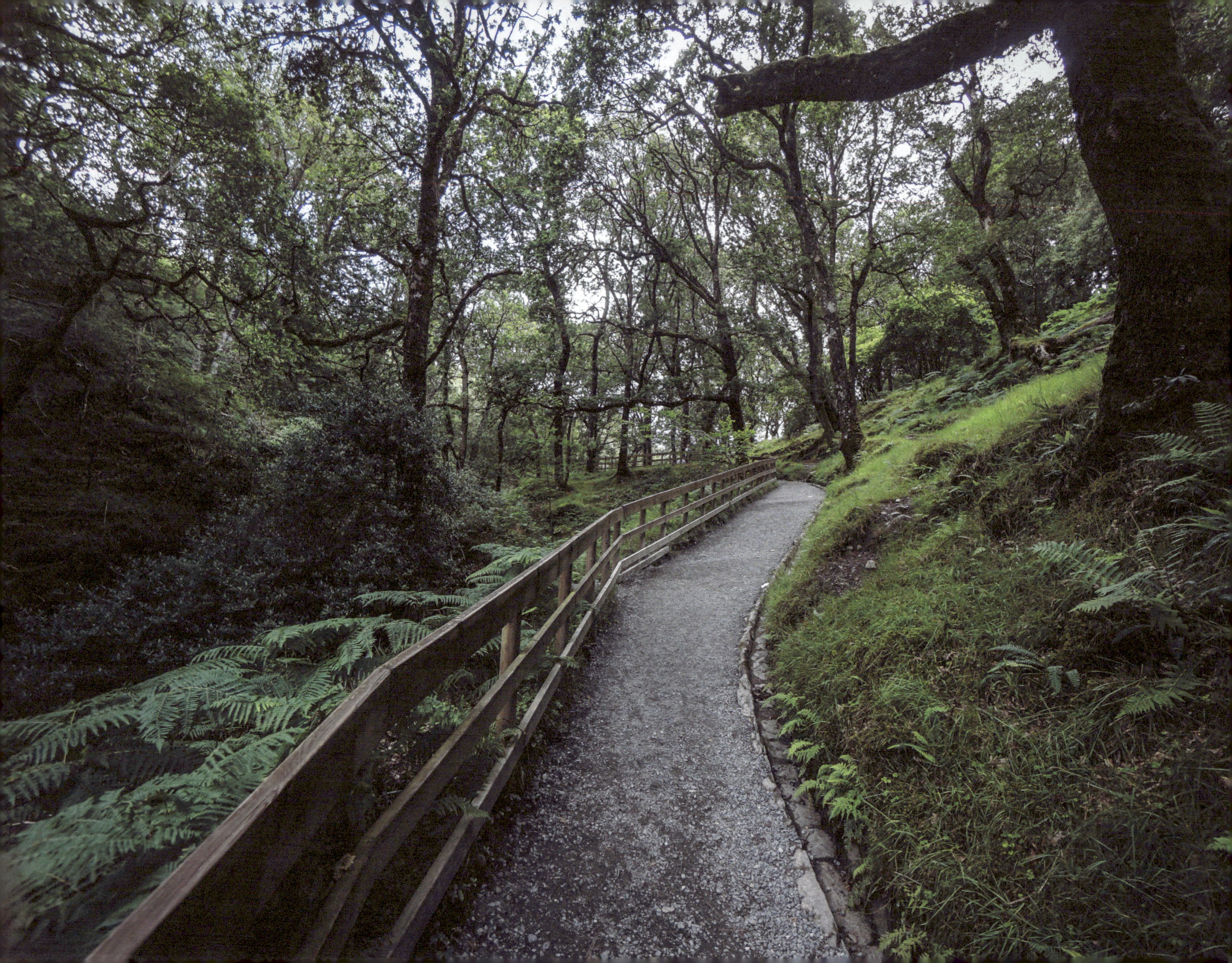

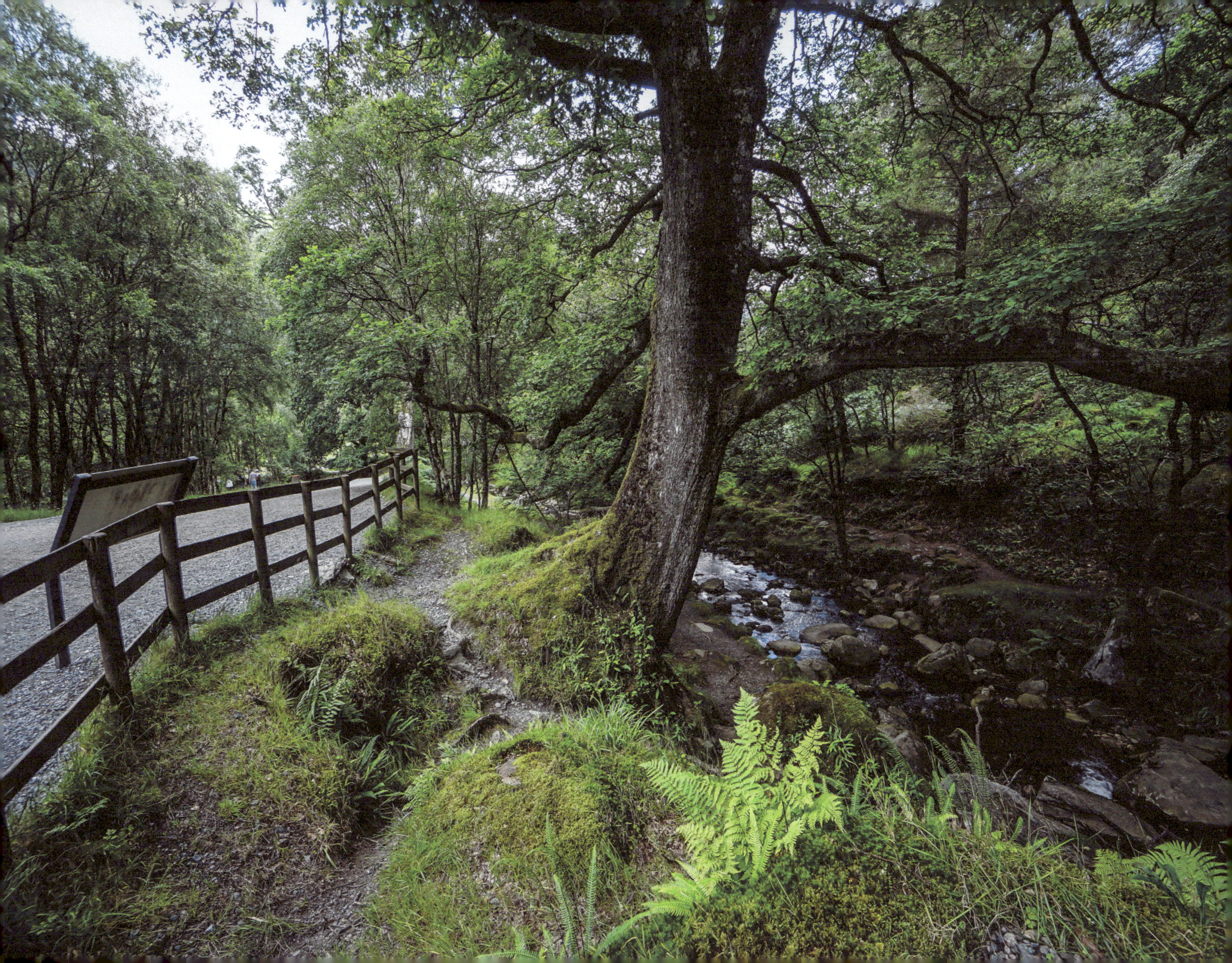

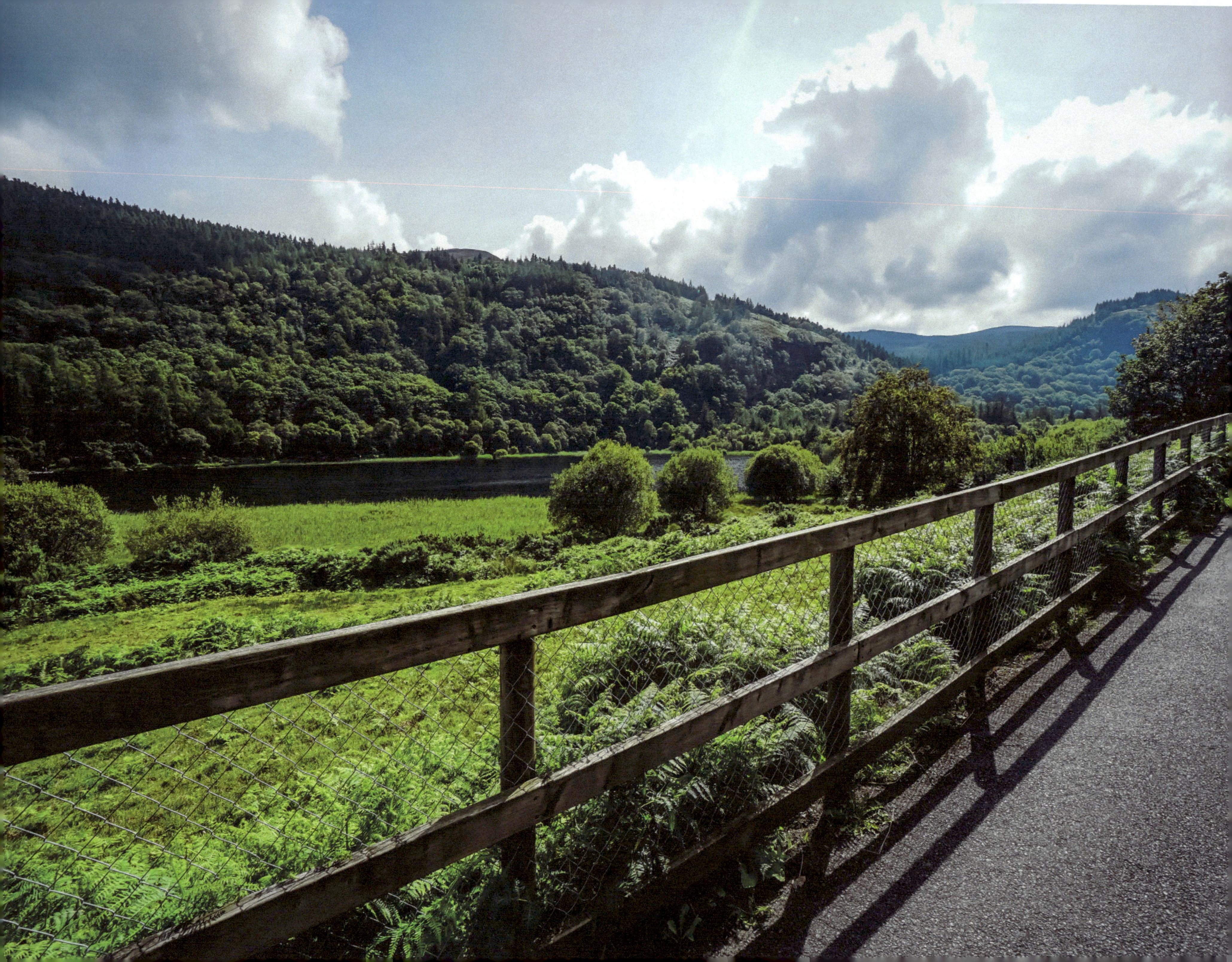

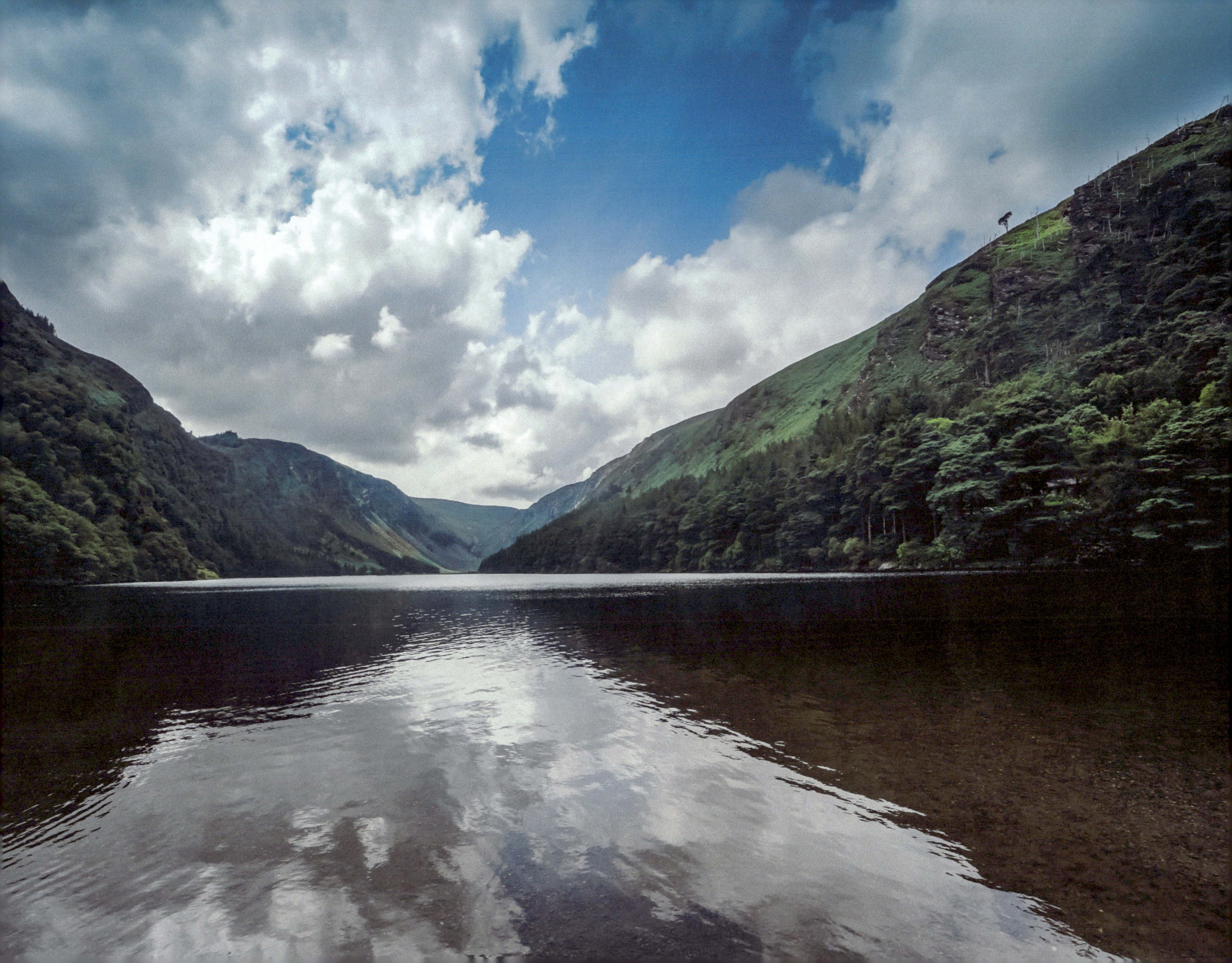

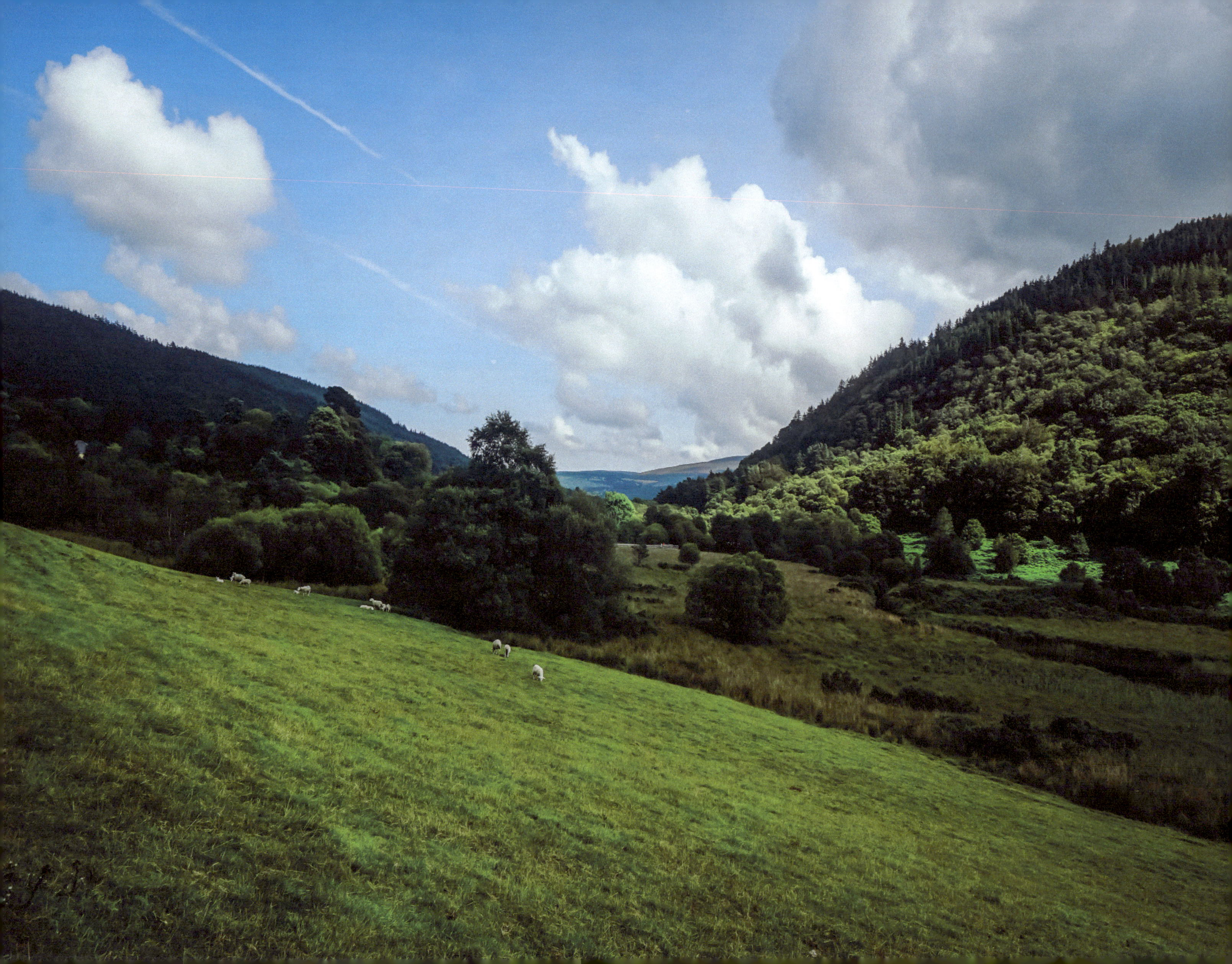

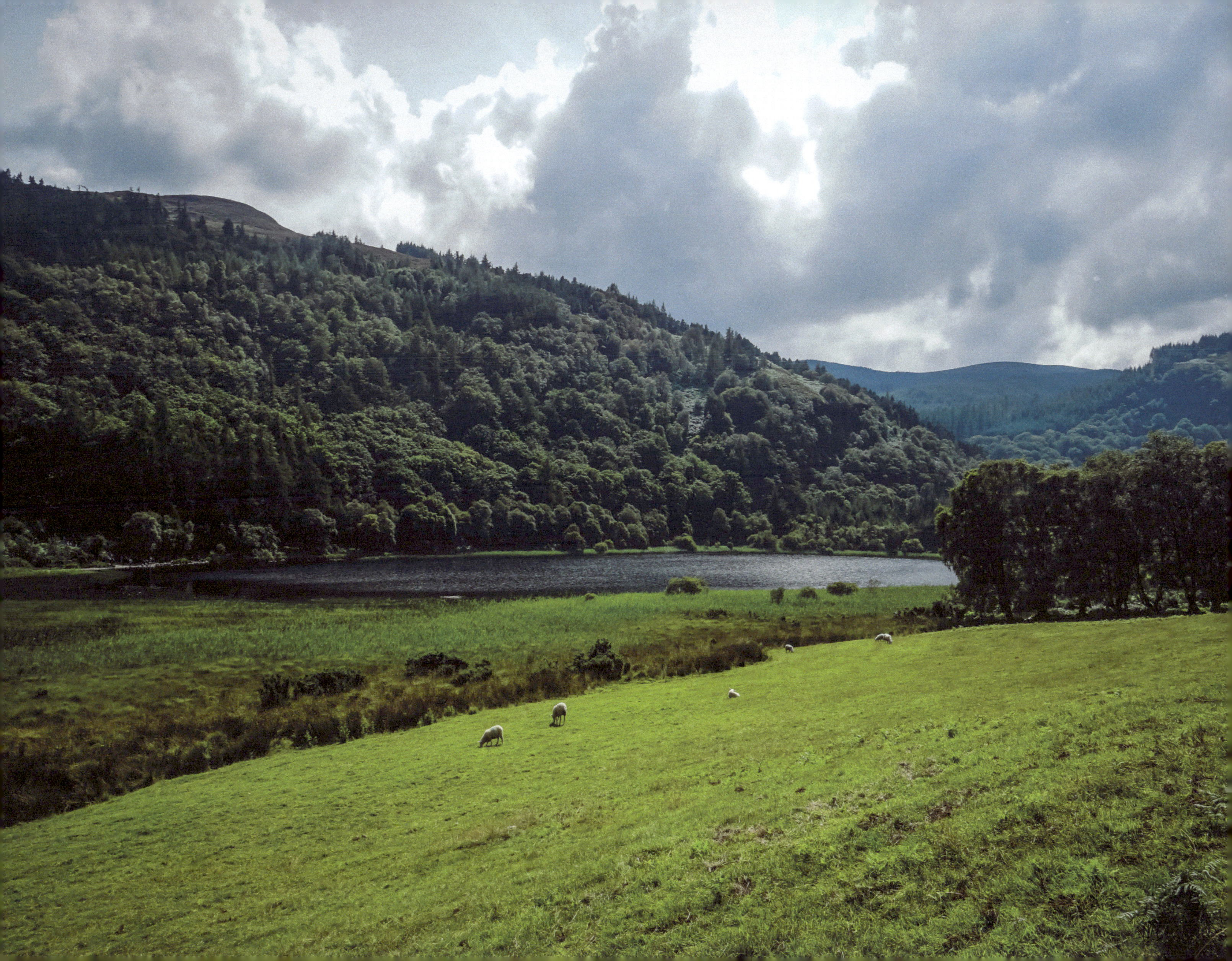

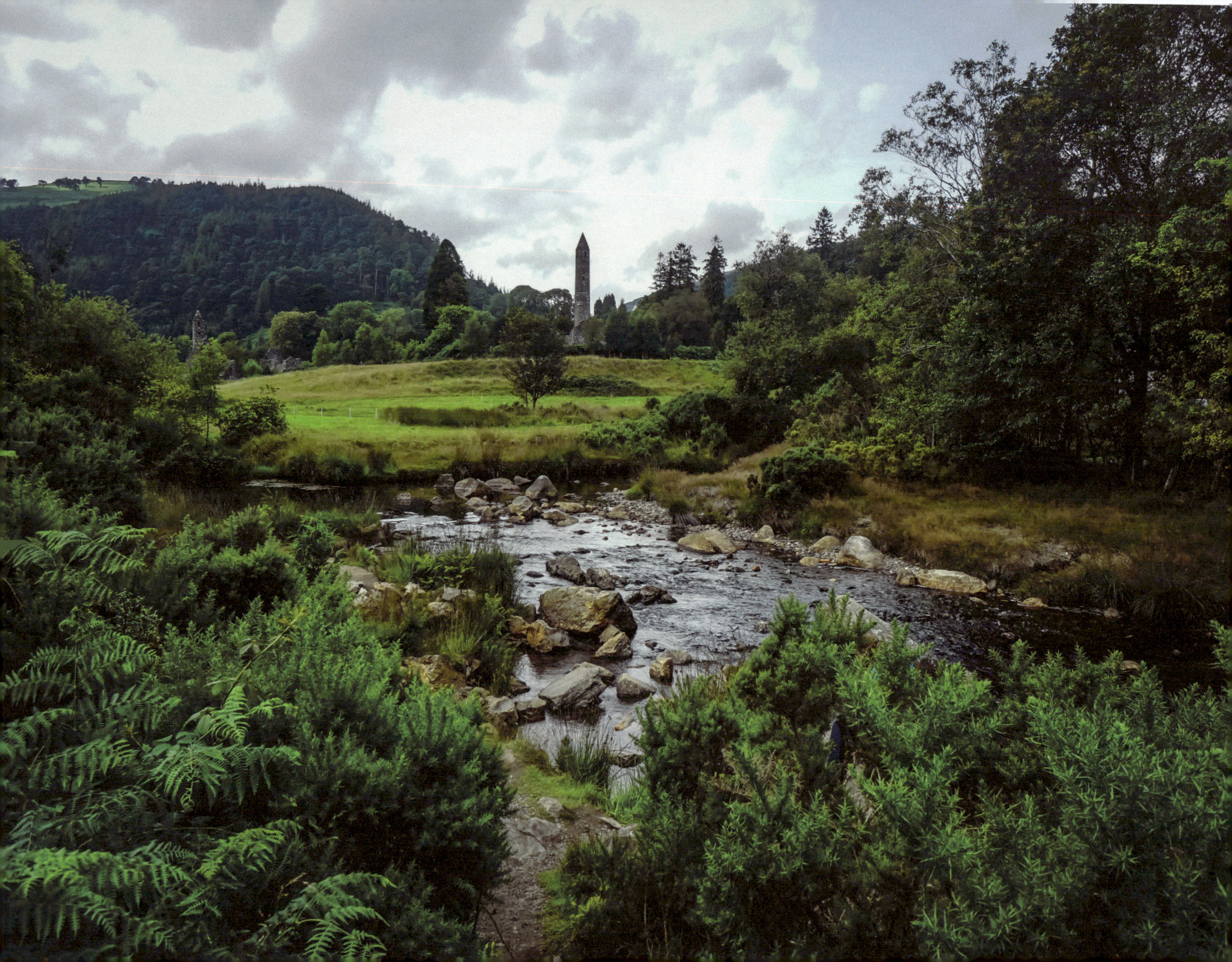

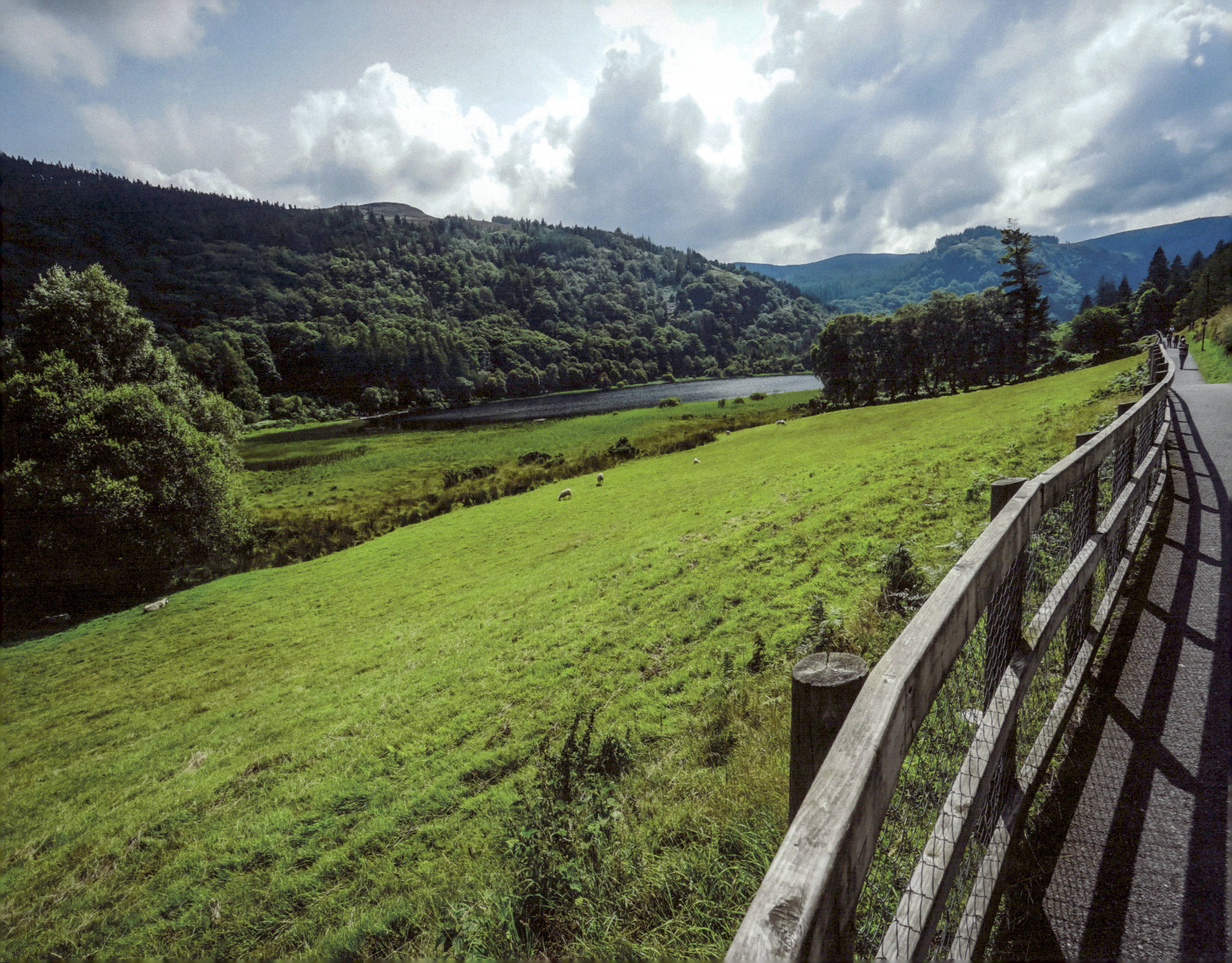

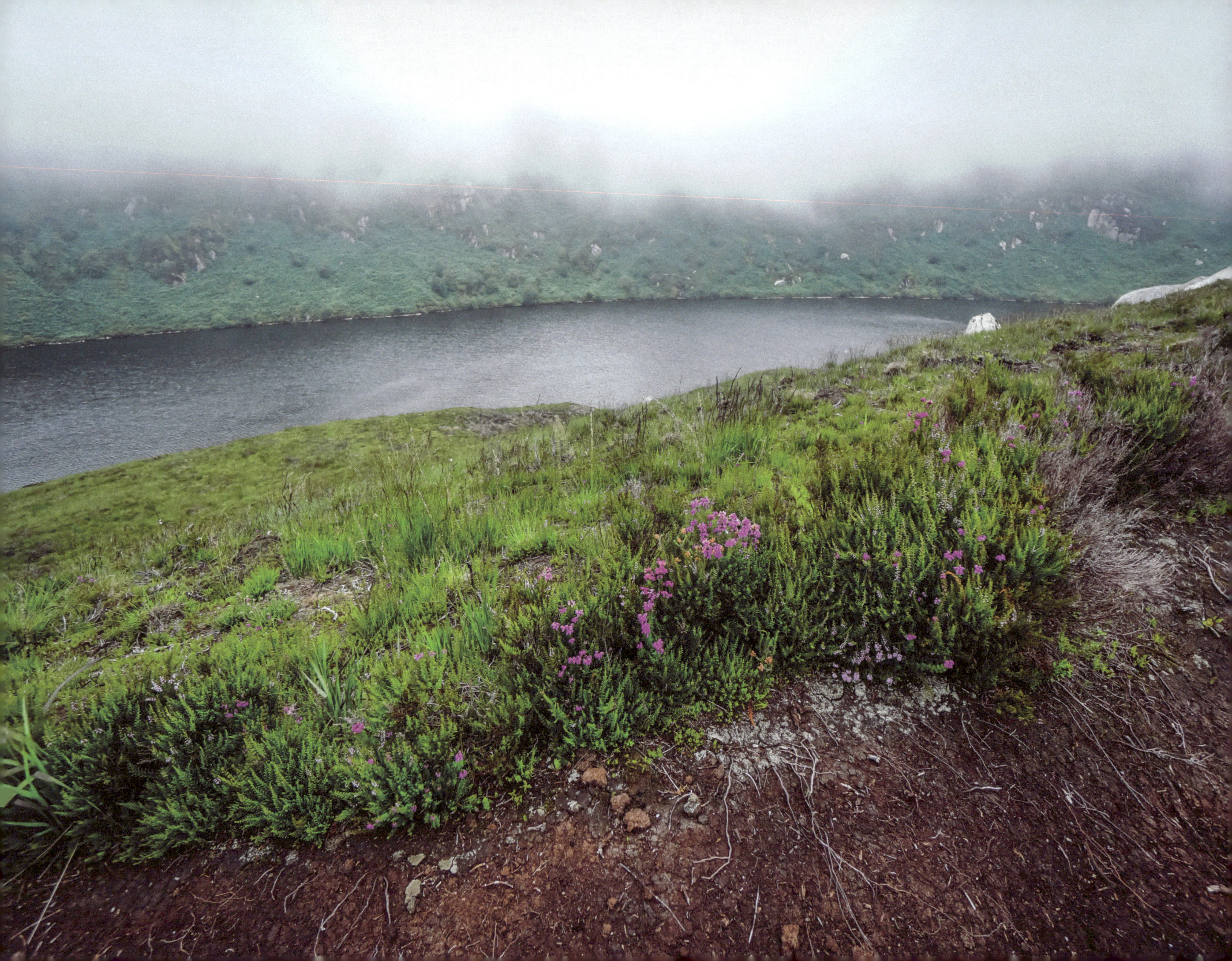

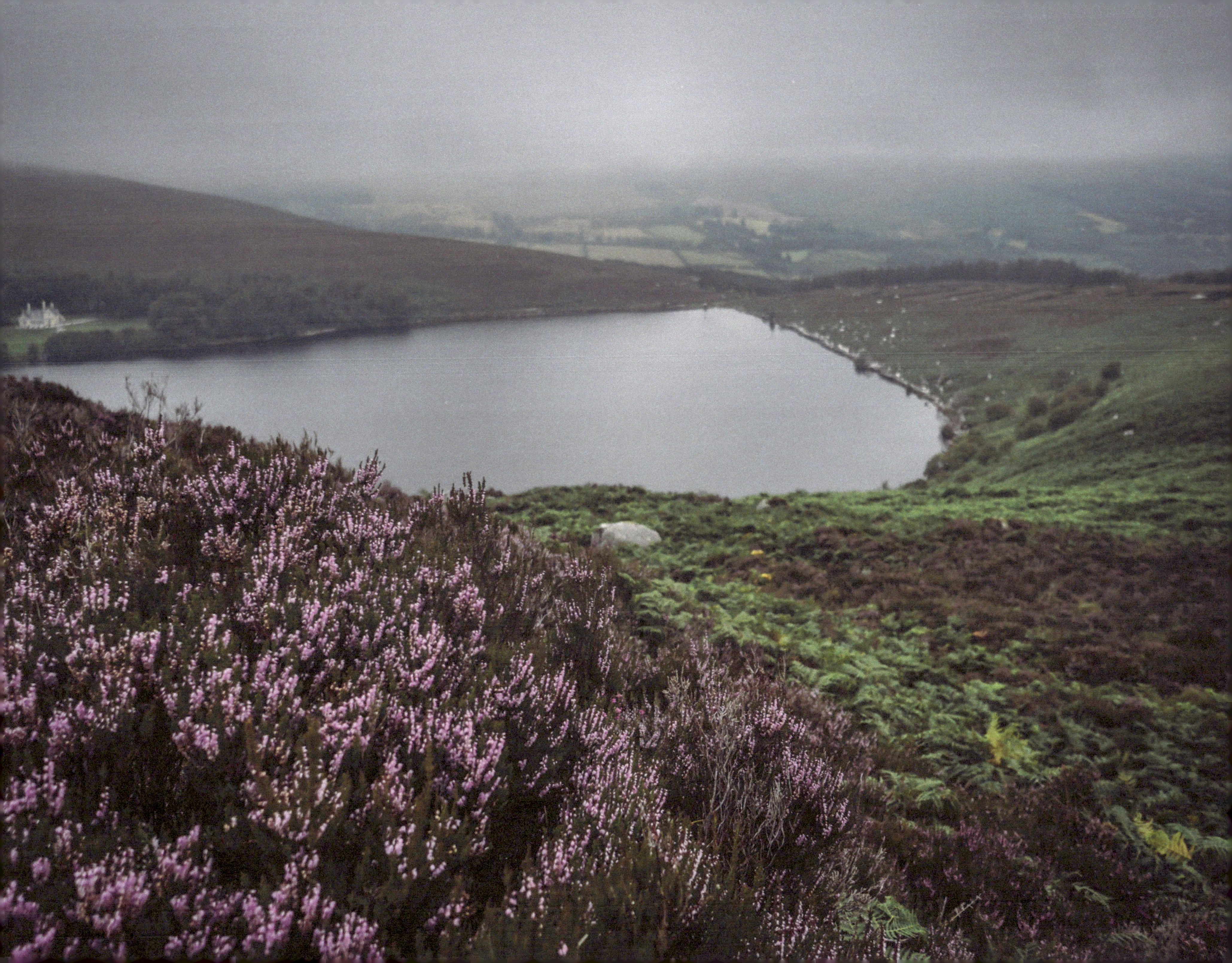

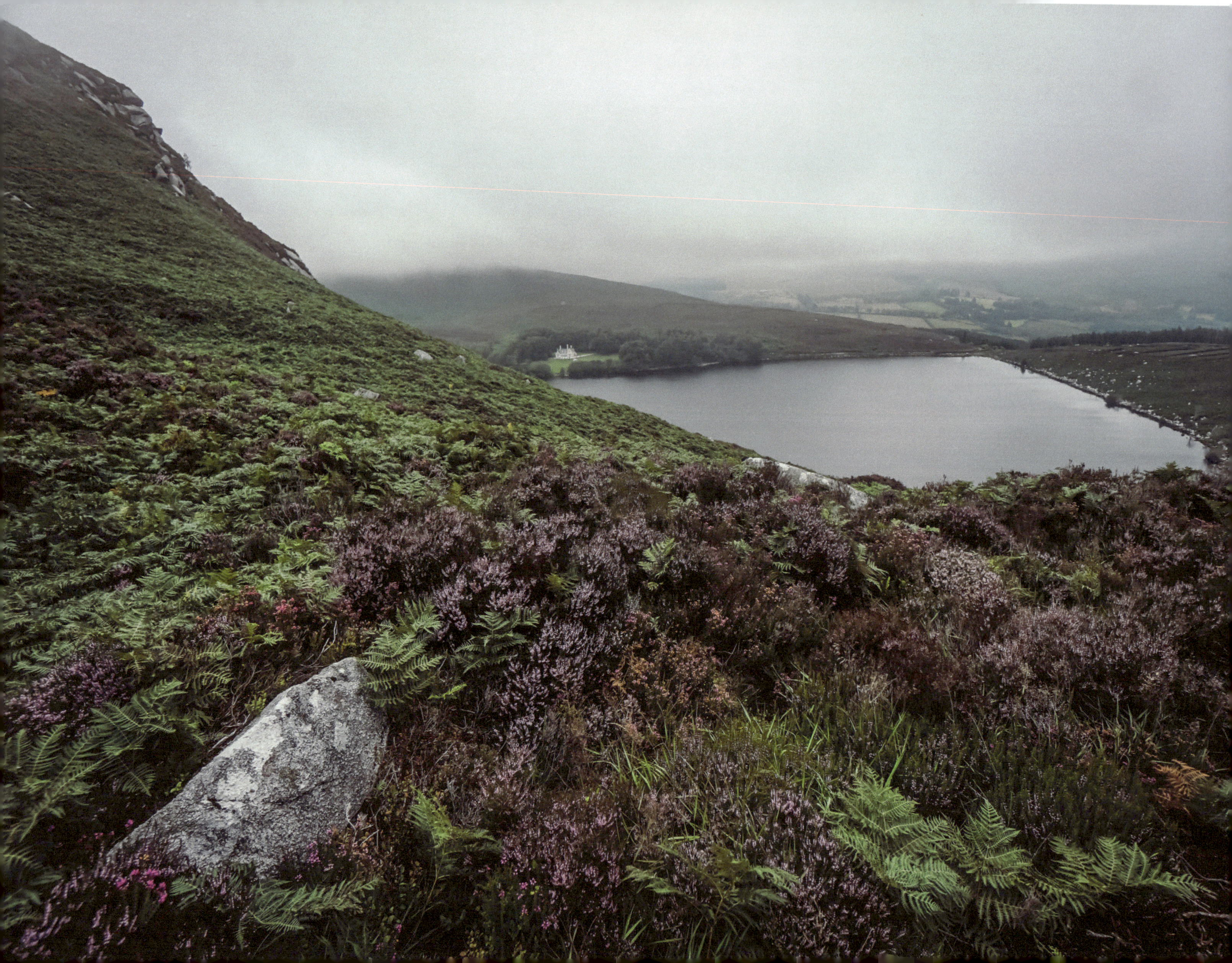

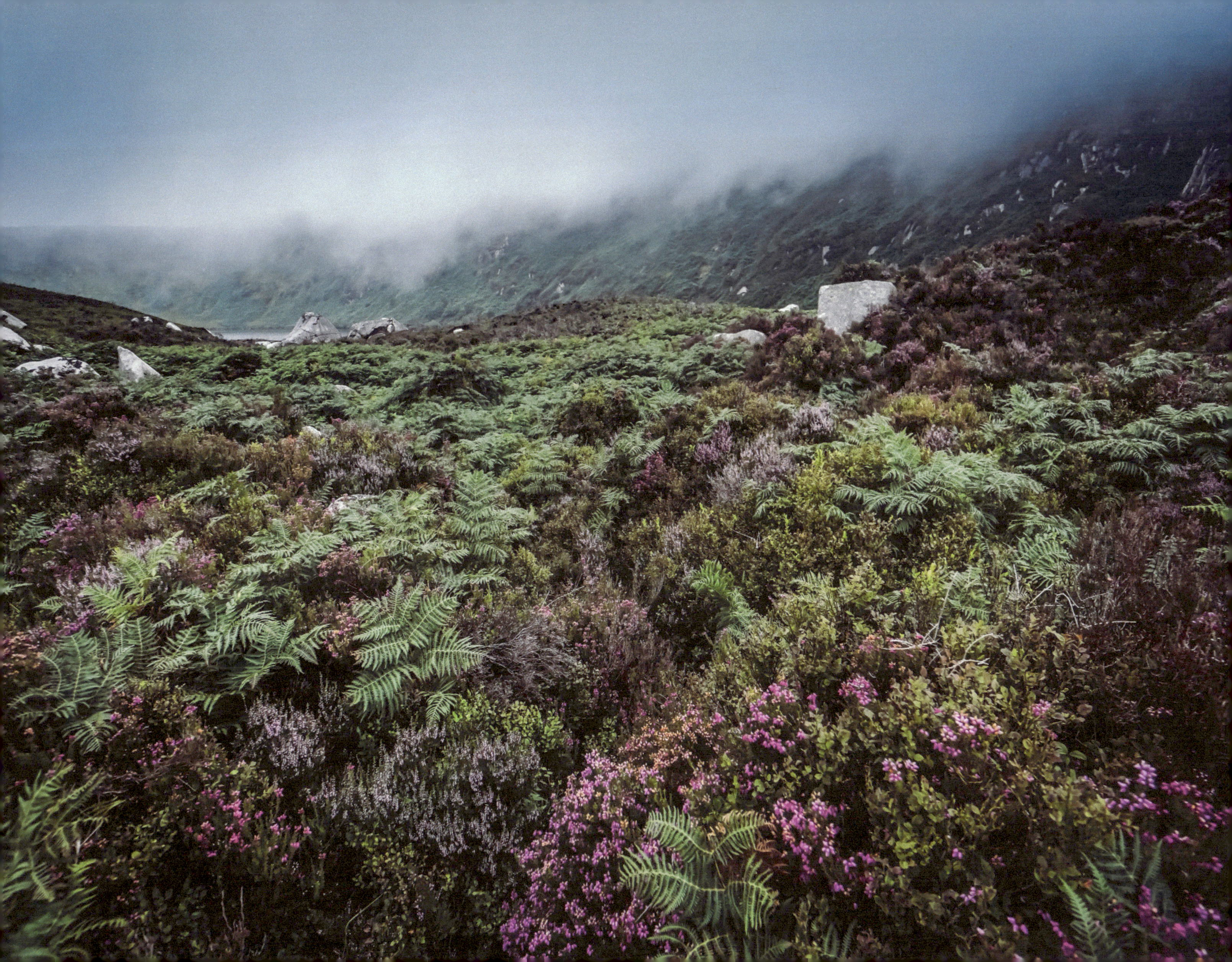

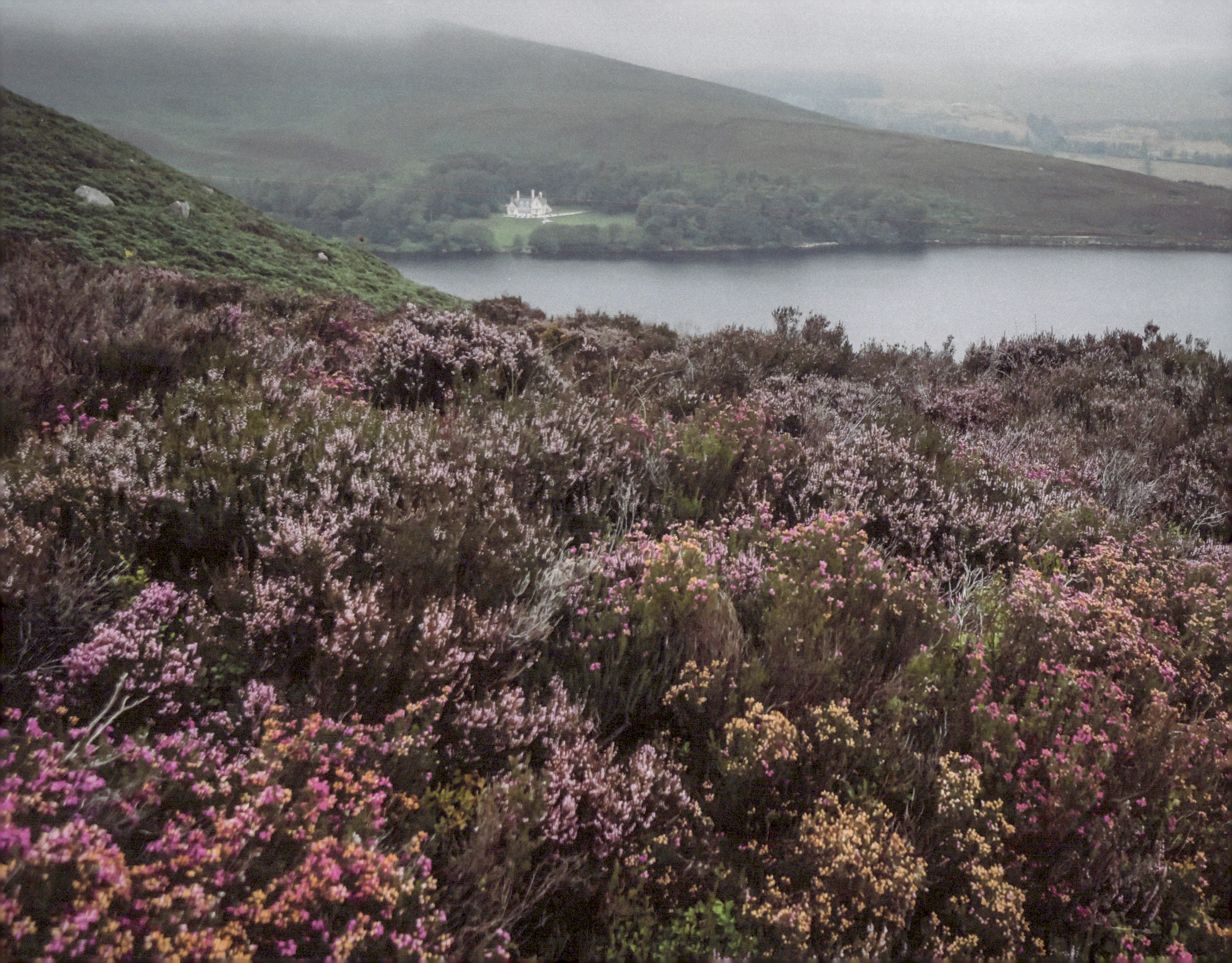

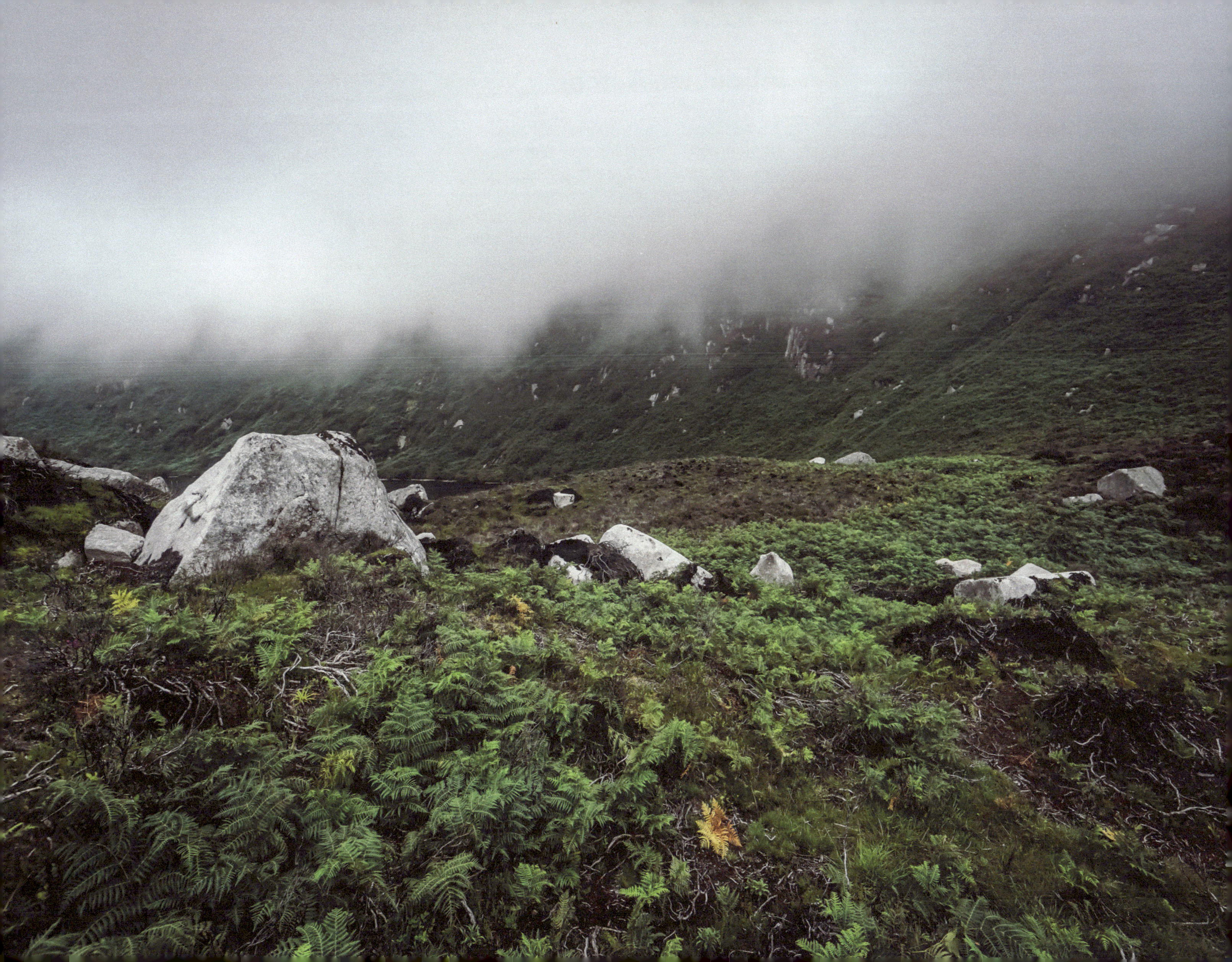

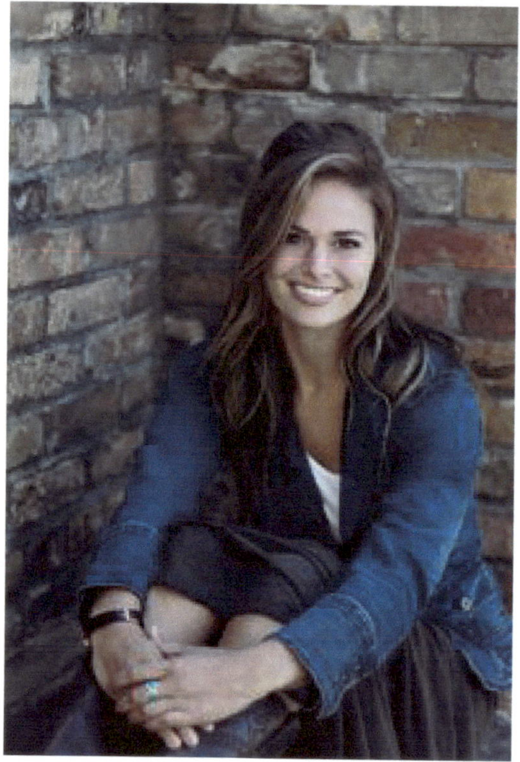

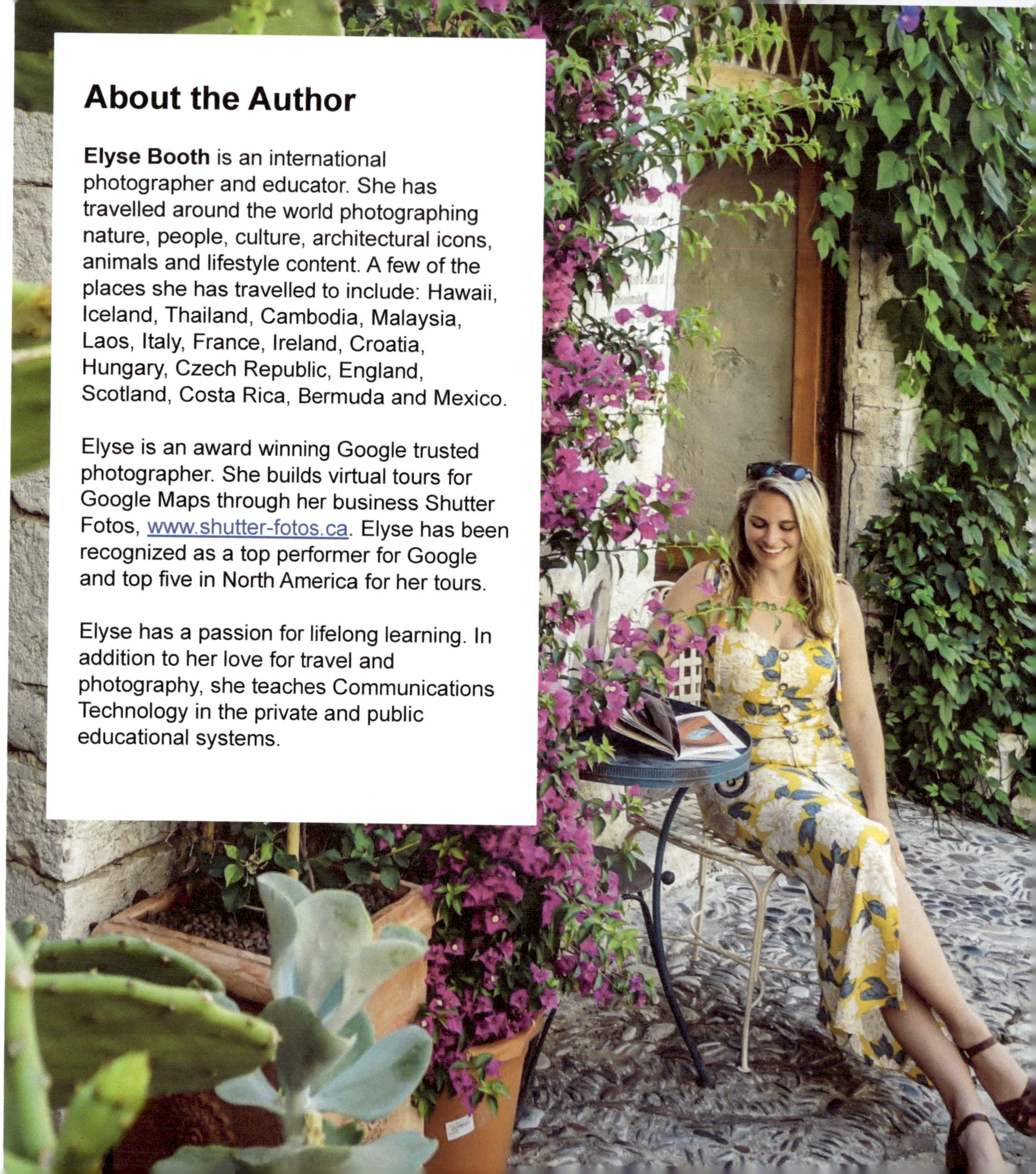

About the Author

Elyse Booth is an international photographer and educator. She has travelled around the world photographing nature, people, culture, architectural icons, animals and lifestyle content. A few of the places she has travelled to include: Hawaii, Iceland, Thailand, Cambodia, Malaysia, Laos, Italy, France, Ireland, Croatia, Hungary, Czech Republic, England, Scotland, Costa Rica, Bermuda and Mexico.

Elyse is an award winning Google trusted photographer. She builds virtual tours for Google Maps through her business Shutter Fotos, www.shutter-fotos.ca. Elyse has been recognized as a top performer for Google and top five in North America for her tours.

Elyse has a passion for lifelong learning. In addition to her love for travel and photography, she teaches Communications Technology in the private and public educational systems.

Social Media & Contact

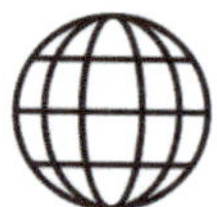 www.shutter-fotos.ca

 elyse@shutter-fotos.ca

 @shutter_fotos

 @ShutterFotos

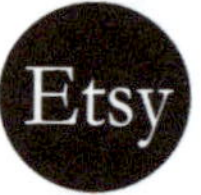 @FotoBoothphotography